Parish Mass Book

Year A Part 2

McCRIMMONS
Great Wakering Essex

First published in Great Britain in 1975 by
MAYHEW-MCCRIMMON LTD

This edition 1999
Published by
MCCRIMMON PUBLISHING CO LTD
10-12 High Street, Great Wakering, Essex SS3 0EQ
Tel: (01702) 218956 Fax: (01702) 216082
Email: mccrimmons@dial.pipex.com

Cum originali concordat
Nihil obstat
Imprimatur

John P. Dewis
Brian O'Higgins, D. D.
C. D. Creede, V. G.
Brentwood.

ISBN 0 85597 013 8

Acknowledgements
English translation of the Roman Missal copyright © 1973, 1974, International Committee on English in the Liturgy, Inc. All rights reserved.
English translation of the Eucharistic Prayers for Masses with Children and Eucharistic Prayers for Masses of Reconciliation, copyright © 1975, International Committee on English in the Liturgy, Inc. All rights reserved.
The alternative translations of the Antiphons and Prayers are © copyright by the National Liturgical Commission for England and Wales.
The scripture texts are taken from the Jerusalem Bible Version of the Scriptures, copyrights © in 1966, 1967 and 1968 by Darton, Longman and Todd Ltd and Doubleday and Co Inc, and used by permission. The version of the Psalms is that translated from the Hebrew by The Grail, copyright © 1963, The Grail (England) and published by William Collins and Sons Ltd in *The Psalms: A New Translation*. Used by permission.

Cover design: Paul Shuttleworth
Typeset in Plantin
Printed by Permanent Typesetting & Printing Co. Ltd., Hong Kong

Contents

The Order of Mass

INTRODUCTORY RITES

ENTRANCE PROCESSION

When the people have assembled the priest and ministers go to the altar. A hymn may be sung, otherwise the Entrance Antiphon is recited.

▶ Proper of the Day

GREETING

Everyone makes the sign of the cross as the priest says:
In the name of the Father, and of the Son, and of the Holy Spirit.
Amen.

The priest greets the people in one of the following ways, or in similar words.

1　The grace of our Lord Jesus Christ
　　and the love of God
　　and the fellowship of the Holy Spirit be with you all.
　　And also with you.

2　The grace and peace of God our Father and
　　the Lord Jesus Christ be with you.
　　Blessed be God, the Father of our Lord Jesus Christ. *or* **And also with you.**

3　The Lord be with you. **And also with you.**

PENITENTIAL RITE

The priest invites the people to repentance in these or similar words:

My brothers and sisters,
to prepare ourselves to celebrate the sacred mysteries,
let us call to mind our sins.

After a brief silence there follows one of the forms of the Penitential Rite.

1　**I confess to almighty God,**
　　and to you, my brothers and sisters,
　　that I have sinned through my own fault
　　　　all strike their breast
　　in my thoughts and in my words,
　　in what I have done,
　　and in what I have failed to do;
　　and I ask blessed Mary, ever virgin,
　　all the angels and saints,
　　and you, my brothers and sisters,
　　to pray for me to the Lord our God.

May almighty God have mercy on us,
forgive us our sins
and bring us to everlasting life. **Amen.**

Lord, have mercy.   **Lord, have mercy.**
Christ, have mercy.   **Christ, have mercy.**
Lord, have mercy.   **Lord, have mercy.**

▶ Gloria: below

2 Lord, we have sinned against you:
Lord, have mercy.
Lord, have mercy.
Lord, show us your mercy and love.
And grant us your salvation.
May almighty God have mercy on us,
forgive us our sins,
and bring us to everlasting life. **Amen.**

Lord, have mercy.   **Lord, have mercy.**
Christ, have mercy.   **Christ, have mercy.**
Lord, have mercy.   **Lord, have mercy.**

▶ Gloria: below

3 You were sent to heal the contrite:* Lord, have mercy.
Lord, have mercy.
You came to call sinners: Christ, have mercy.
Christ, have mercy.
You plead for us at the right hand of the Father: Lord, have mercy.
Lord, have mercy.
May almighty God have mercy on us, forgive us our sins,
and bring us to everlasting life. **Amen.**

* Other invocations may be used.

THE GLORIA

This hymn of praise is omitted in Advent and Lent.

Glory to God in the highest,
  and peace to his people on earth.

Lord God, heavenly King,
almighty God and Father,
  we worship you, we give you thanks,
  we praise you for your glory.

Lord Jesus Christ, only Son of the Father,
Lord God, Lamb of God,
you take away the sin of the world:

have mercy on us;
you are seated at the right hand of
  the Father:
receive our prayer.

For you alone are the Holy One,
you alone are the Lord,
you alone are the Most High,
  Jesus Christ,
  with the Holy Spirit,
  in the glory of God the Father. Amen.

OPENING PRAYER

▶ Proper of the Day

In this prayer the priest 'collects' the intentions of all present. All respond **Amen.**

Liturgy of the Word

In the Liturgy of the Word (see Proper of the Day) God speaks anew to his people and they respond in prayer. After the readings and homily all stand for the Creed.

CREED
We believe in one God,
  the Father, the Almighty,
  maker of heaven and earth,
  of all that is, seen and unseen.

We believe in one Lord, Jesus Christ,
  the only Son of God,
  eternally begotten of the Father,
  God from God, Light from Light,
  true God from true God,
  begotten, not made,
  of one Being with the Father.
  Through him all things were made.
  For us men and for our salvation
  he came down from heaven: *all bow*
by the power of the Holy Spirit
  he became incarnate from the Virgin Mary,
  and was made man.
For our sake he was crucified under Pontius Pilate;
  he suffered death and was buried.
  On the third day he rose again
    in accordance with the Scriptures;
  he ascended into heaven
    and is seated at the right hand of the Father.
  He will come again in glory to judge the living and the dead,
  and his kingdom will have no end.

We believe in the Holy Spirit, the Lord, the giver of life,
  who proceeds from the Father and the Son.
  With the Father and the Son he is worshipped and glorified.
  He has spoken through the Prophets.
  We believe in one holy catholic and apostolic Church.
  We acknowledge one baptism for the forgiveness of sins.
  We look for the resurrection of the dead.
  and the life of the world to come. Amen.

PRAYER OF THE FAITHFUL
The whole assembly now prays for the needs of the world, the Church and the local community. A series of intentions is presented to guide the prayer, after each of which all say **Hear our prayer** *or* **Lord, graciously hear us** *or any other customary phrase. A prayer by the priest concludes and all answer* **Amen.**

The Liturgy of the Eucharist

Having listened to the 'great works of God' in the scriptures, we give thanks in the way Christ taught us, following his command to 'take, bless, break and eat' in memory of Him.

PREPARATION OF THE ALTAR AND GIFTS

The offerings are brought to the altar. The assembly may sing a hymn, which may continue while the priest says the following prayers in silence. If there is no hymn the priest may say the prayers aloud and all make the response.
Blessed are you, Lord, God of all creation.
Through your goodness we have this bread to offer,
which earth has given and human hands have made.
It will become for us the bread of life.
Blessed be God for ever.

The priest says quietly:
By the mystery of this water and wine may we come to share in the divinity of Christ, who humbled himself to share in our humanity.

He continues aloud:
Blessed are you, Lord, God of all creation.
Through your goodness we have this wine to offer,
fruit of the vine and work of human hands.
It will become our spiritual drink.
Blessed be God for ever.

The priest says quietly:
Lord God, we ask you to receive us and be pleased with the sacrifice we offer you with humble and contrite hearts.

The priest washes his hands, saying quietly:
Lord, wash away my iniquity;
cleanse me from my sin.

He invites the people to prayer:
Pray, brethren, that our sacrifice
        (*or* Pray, brethren, that my sacrifice and yours)
may be acceptable to God the almighty Father.
May the Lord accept the sacrifice at your hands,
for the praise and glory of his name,
for our good, and the good of all his Church.

PRAYER OVER THE GIFTS   ▶ Proper of the Day
This second 'presidential prayer' concludes the Preparation of the Altar and Gifts.

THE EUCHARISTIC PRAYER

In the Eucharistic Prayer the whole assembly unites to praise and give thanks to God and to offer sacrifice.

THE PREFACE

The Preface is the first, variable, section of the Eucharistic Prayer. Unless a particular day has a special Preface, one is taken from the following selection. Eucharistic Prayer 2 has its own Preface (page 16) for which another may be substituted. Eucharistic Prayer 4, however, has an invariable Preface.

▶ Eucharistic Prayer 4: p.17

The Lord be with you. **And also with you.**
Lift up your hearts. **We lift them up to the Lord.**
Let us give thanks to the Lord our God. **It is right to give him thanks and praise.**

SUNDAYS IN ORDINARY TIME 1
Father, all-powerful and ever-living God,
we do well always and everywhere to give you
    thanks
through Jesus Christ our Lord.

Through his cross and resurrection
he freed us from sin and death
and called us to the glory that has made us
a chosen race, a royal priesthood,
a holy nation, a people set apart.

Everywhere we proclaim your mighty works
for you have called us out of darkness
into your own wonderful light.

And so, with all the choirs of angels in heaven
we proclaim your glory
and join in their unending hymn of praise:

SUNDAYS IN ORDINARY TIME 2
Father, all-powerful and ever-living God,
we do well always and everywhere to give you
    thanks
through Jesus Christ our Lord.

Out of love for sinful man,
he humbled himself to be born of the Virgin.

By suffering on the cross
he freed us from unending death,
and by rising from the dead
he gave us eternal life.

And so, with all the choirs of angels in heaven
we proclaim your glory
and join in their unending hymn of praise:

SUNDAYS IN ORDINARY TIME 3
Father, all-powerful and ever-living God,
we do well always and everywhere to give you
    thanks.

We see your infinite power
in your loving plan of salvation.
You came to our rescue by your power as God,
but you wanted us to be saved by one like us.
Man refused your friendship,
but man himself was to restore it
through Jesus Christ our Lord.

Through him the angels of heaven offer their
    prayer of adoration
as they rejoice in your presence for ever.
May our voices be one with theirs
in their triumphant hymn of praise:

SUNDAYS IN ORDINARY TIME 4
Father, all-powerful and ever-living God,
we do well always and everywhere to give you
    thanks
through Jesus Christ our Lord.

By his birth we are reborn.
In his suffering we are freed from sin.
By his rising from the dead we rise to everlasting
    life.
In his return to you in glory
we enter into your heavenly kingdom.

And so we join the angels and the saints
as they sing their unending hymn of praise:

SUNDAYS IN ORDINARY TIME 5
Father, all-powerful and ever-living God,
we do well always and everywhere to give you
 thanks.

All things are of your making,
all times and seasons obey your laws,
but you chose to create man in your own image,
setting him over the whole world in all its
 wonder.
You made man the steward of creation,
to praise you day by day for the marvels of your
 wisdom and power,
through Jesus Christ our Lord.

We praise you, Lord, with all the angels and
 saints
in their song of joy:

SUNDAYS IN ORDINARY TIME 6
Father, all-powerful and ever-living God,
we do well always and everywhere to give you
 thanks.

In you we live and move and have our being.
Each day you show us a Father's love;
your Holy Spirit dwelling within us,
gives us on earth the hope of unending joy.

Your gift of the Spirit,
who raised Jesus from the dead,
is the foretaste and promise
of the paschal feast of heaven.

With thankful praise,
in company with the angels,
we glorify the wonders of your power:

SUNDAYS IN ORDINARY TIME 7
Father, all-powerful and ever-living God,
we do well always and everywhere to give you
 thanks.

So great was your love
that you gave us your Son as our Redeemer.
You sent him as one like ourselves,
though free from sin,
that you might see and love in us
what you see and love in Christ.

Your gifts of grace, lost by disobedience,
are now restored by the obedience of your Son.

We praise you, Lord, with all the angels and
 saints
in their song of joy:

SUNDAYS IN ORDINARY TIME 8
Father, all-powerful and ever-living God,
we do well always and everywhere to give you
 thanks.

When your children sinned
and wandered far from your friendship,
you reunited them with yourself
through the blood of your Son
and the power of the Holy Spirit.

You gather them into your Church,
to be one as you, Father, are one
with your Son and the Holy Spirit.
You call them to be your people,
to praise your wisdom in all your works.
You make them the body of Christ
and the dwelling-place of the Holy Spirit.

In our joy we sing to your glory
with all the choirs of angels:

**Holy, holy, holy Lord, God of power and might,
heaven and earth are full of your glory.
 Hosanna in the highest.
Blessed is he who comes in the name of the Lord.
 Hosanna in the highest.**

▶ Eucharistic Prayer 1: p.10
▶ Eucharistic Prayer 2: p.13
▶ Eucharistic Prayer 3: p.15

Eucharistic Prayer 1 (The Roman Canon)

We come to you, Father,
with praise and thanksgiving,
through Jesus Christ your Son.
Through him we ask you to accept and bless
these gifts we offer you in sacrifice.
We offer them for your holy catholic Church,
watch over it, Lord, and guide it;
grant it peace and unity throughout the world.
We offer them for *N.* our Pope,
for *N.* our bishop,
and for all who hold and teach the catholic faith
that comes to us from the apostles.

Remember, Lord, your people,
especially those for whom we now pray, *N.* and *N.*
Remember all of us gathered here before you.
You know how firmly we believe in you
and dedicate ourselves to you.
We offer you this sacrifice of praise
for ourselves and those who are dear to us.
We pray to you, our living and true God,
for our well-being and redemption.

Commemoration
of the Living

In union with the whole Church*
we honour Mary,
the ever-virgin mother of Jesus Christ our Lord and God.
We honour Joseph, her husband,
the apostles and martyrs
Peter and Paul, Andrew,
  (James, John, Thomas,
  James, Philip,
  Bartholomew, Matthew, Simon and Jude;
  we honour Linus, Cletus, Clement, Sixtus,
  Cornelius, Cyprian, Lawrence, Chrysogonus,
  John and Paul, Cosmas and Damian)
and all the saints.
May their merits and prayers
gain us your constant help and protection.
(Through Christ our Lord. Amen.)

In union with
the Church

---

* *Pentecost*
 In union with the whole Church
we celebrate the day of Pentecost
when the Holy Spirit appeared to the apostles
in the form of countless tongues.
We honour Mary ...

Father, accept this offering
from your whole family.
Grant us your peace in this life,
save us from final damnation,
and count us among those you have chosen.

*For acceptance
of the offering*

Bless and approve our offering;
make it acceptable to you,
an offering in spirit and in truth.
Let it become for us
the body and blood of Jesus Christ,
your only Son, our Lord.

*The Last Supper narrative
and the Consecration*

The day before he suffered
he took bread in his sacred hands
and looking up to heaven,
to you, his almighty Father,
he gave you thanks and praise.
He broke the bread,
gave it to his disciples, and said:

TAKE THIS, ALL OF YOU, AND EAT IT:
THIS IS MY BODY WHICH WILL BE GIVEN UP FOR YOU.

When supper was ended, he took the cup.
Again he gave you thanks and praise,
gave the cup to his disciples, and said:

TAKE THIS, ALL OF YOU, AND DRINK FROM IT:
THIS IS THE CUP OF MY BLOOD,
THE BLOOD OF THE NEW AND EVERLASTING COVENANT.
IT WILL BE SHED FOR YOU AND FOR ALL
SO THAT SINS MAY BE FORGIVEN.
DO THIS IN MEMORY OF ME.

The priest (or the deacon, if there is one) says or sings:
Let us proclaim the mystery of faith:

*Memorial
Acclamation*

1 **Christ has died,
   Christ is risen,
   Christ will come again.**

Alternative acclamations

2 **Dying you destroyed our death,
   rising you restored our life.
   Lord Jesus, come in glory.**

3 **When we eat this bread and drink this cup,
   we proclaim your death, Lord Jesus,
   until you come in glory.**

4 **Lord, by your cross and resurrection
   you have set us free.
   You are the Saviour of the world.**

Father, we celebrate the memory of Christ, your Son.
We, your people and your ministers,
recall his passion,
his resurrection from the dead,
and his ascension into glory;
and from the many gifts you have given us
we offer to you, God of glory and majesty,
this holy and perfect sacrifice:
the bread of life and the cup of eternal salvation.

Look with favour on these offerings
and accept them as once you accepted the gifts of your servant Abel,
the sacrifice of Abraham, our father in faith,
and the bread and wine offered by your priest Melchisedech.

Almighty God,
we pray that your angel may take this sacrifice to your altar in heaven.
Then, as we receive from this altar
the sacred body and blood of your Son,
let us be filled with every grace and blessing.
(Through Christ our Lord. Amen.)

Remember, Lord, those who have died   *Commemoration*
and have gone before us marked with the sign of faith,   *of the Dead*
especially those for whom we now pray, *N.* and *N.*
May these, and all who sleep in Christ,
find in your presence
light, happiness, and peace.
(Through Christ our Lord. Amen.)

For ourselves, too, we ask
some share in the fellowship of your apostles and martyrs,   *For ourselves*
with John the Baptist, Stephen, Matthias, Barnabas,
(Ignatius, Alexander, Marcellinus, Peter, Felicity, Perpetua,
Agatha, Lucy, Agnes, Cecilia, Anastasia)
and all the saints.

Though we are sinners,
we trust in your mercy and love.
Do not consider what we truly deserve,
but grant us your forgiveness.

Through Christ our Lord you give us all these gifts.
You fill them with life and goodness,
you bless them and make them holy.

Through him,   *Doxology and*
with him,   *Great Amen*

in him,
in the unity of the Holy Spirit,
all glory and honour is yours,
almighty Father,
for ever and ever.
Amen.

▶ Continue on p.20

Eucharistic Prayer 2

(This Preface may be substituted by one from pages 8-9 or a proper preface)

The Lord be with you.	**And also with you.**
Lift up your hearts.	**We lift them up to the Lord.**
Let us give thanks to the Lord our God.	**It is right to give him thanks and praise.**

Father, it is our duty and our salvation,
always and everywhere
to give you thanks
through your beloved Son, Jesus Christ.
He is the Word through whom you made the universe,
the Saviour you sent to redeem us.
By the power of the Holy Spirit
he took flesh and was born of the Virgin Mary.

For our sake he opened his arms on the cross;
he put an end to death
and revealed the resurrection.
He fulfilled your will
and won for you a holy people.
And so we join the angels and the saints
in proclaiming your glory
as we sing (say):

Holy, holy, holy Lord ...

Lord, you are holy indeed,   *Invocation of*
the fountain of all holiness.   *the Spirit*
Let your Spirit come upon these gifts to make them holy,
so that they may become for us
the body and blood of our Lord, Jesus Christ.

Before he was given up to death,   *The Last Supper narrative*
a death he freely accepted,   *and Consecration*
he took bread and gave you thanks.
He broke the bread,
gave it to his disciples, and said:

TAKE THIS, ALL OF YOU, AND EAT IT:
THIS IS MY BODY WHICH WILL BE GIVEN UP FOR YOU.

When supper was ended, he took the cup.
Again he gave you thanks and praise, gave the cup to his disciples, and said:
TAKE THIS, ALL OF YOU, AND DRINK FROM IT:
THIS IS THE CUP OF MY BLOOD,
THE BLOOD OF THE NEW AND EVERLASTING COVENANT.

IT WILL BE SHED FOR YOU AND FOR ALL
SO THAT SINS MAY BE FORGIVEN.
DO THIS IN MEMORY OF ME.

The priest (or the deacon, if there is one) says or sings:
Let us proclaim the mystery of faith: *Memorial Acclamation*
1   **Christ has died,**
    Christ is risen,
    Christ will come again.

Alternative acclamations
2   **Dying you destroyed our death,**   3   **When we eat this bread and drink this cup,**
    rising you restored our life.   **we proclaim your death, Lord Jesus,**
    Lord Jesus, come in glory.   **until you come in glory.**

            4   **Lord, by your cross and resurrection**
                you have set us free.
                You are the Saviour of the world.

In memory of his death and resurrection,
we offer you, Father, this life-giving bread,
this saving cup.
We thank you for counting us worthy
to stand in your presence and serve you.
May all of us who share in the body and blood of Christ
be brought together in unity by the Holy Spirit.

Lord, remember your Church throughout the world;   *Remembrance of the*
make us grow in love,   *Church*
together with *N.* our Pope, *N.* our bishop,   *Living and Dead*
and all the clergy. *

---

* *In Masses for the Dead, the following may be added:*
Remember *N.*, whom you have called from this life.
In baptism he (she) died with Christ:
may he (she) also share his resurrection.

Remember our brothers and sisters
who have gone to their rest
in the hope of rising again;
bring them and all the departed
into the light of your presence.

Have mercy on us all;
make us worthy to share eternal life
with Mary, the virgin Mother of God,
with the apostles, and with all the saints
who have done your will throughout the ages.

May we praise you in union with them,
and give you glory
through your Son, Jesus Christ.

Through him,   *Doxology and*
with him,   *Great Amen*
in him,
in the unity of the Holy Spirit,
all glory and honour is yours,
almighty Father,
for ever and ever.
▶ Continue on p.20
Amen.

Eucharistic Prayer 3

Father, you are holy indeed,
and all creation rightly gives you praise.
All life, all holiness comes from you
through your Son, Jesus Christ our Lord,
by the working of the Holy Spirit.
From age to age you gather a people to yourself,
so that from east to west
a perfect offering may be made
to the glory of your name.

And so, Father, we bring you these gifts.
We ask you to make them holy by the power of your Spirit,   *Invocation of*
that they may become the body and blood   *the Spirit*
of your Son, our Lord Jesus Christ,
at whose command we celebrate this eucharist.

On the night he was betrayed,   *The Last Supper narrative*
he took bread and gave you thanks and praise.   *and Consecration*
He broke the bread, gave it to his disciples, and said:
TAKE THIS, ALL OF YOU, AND EAT IT:
THIS IS MY BODY WHICH WILL BE GIVEN UP FOR YOU.

When supper was ended, he took the cup.
Again he gave you thanks and praise,
gave the cup to his disciples, and said:

TAKE THIS, ALL OF YOU, AND DRINK FROM IT:
THIS IS THE CUP OF MY BLOOD,
THE BLOOD OF THE NEW AND EVERLASTING COVENANT.
IT WILL BE SHED FOR YOU AND FOR ALL
SO THAT SINS MAY BE FORGIVEN.
DO THIS IN MEMORY OF ME.

The priest (or the deacon, if there is one) says or sings:
Let us proclaim the mystery of faith:
1 Christ has died,
Christ is risen,
Christ will come again.

Alternative acclamations

2 Dying you destroyed our death,
rising you restored our life.
Lord Jesus, come in glory.

3 When we eat this bread and drink this cup,
we proclaim your death, Lord Jesus,
until you come in glory.

4 Lord, by your cross and resurrection
you have set us free.
You are the Saviour of the world.

Father, calling to mind the death your Son endured for our salvation,
his glorious resurrection and ascension into heaven,
and ready to greet him when he comes again,
we offer you in thanksgiving this holy and living sacrifice.

Look with favour on your Church's offering,
and see the Victim whose death has reconciled us to yourself.
Grant that we, who are nourished by his body and blood,
may be filled with his Holy Spirit,
and become one body, one spirit in Christ.

May he make us an everlasting gift to you
and enable us to share in the inheritance of your saints,
with Mary, the virgin Mother of God;
with the apostles, the martyrs,
(Saint *N. – the patron saint or saint of the day*) and all your saints,
on whose constant intercession we rely for help.

Lord, may this sacrifice,   *For the Church,*
which has made our peace with you,   *Living and Dead*
advance the peace and salvation of all the world.
Strengthen in faith and love your pilgrim Church on earth;
your servant, Pope *N.*, our bishop *N.*,
and all the bishops,
with the clergy and the entire people your Son has gained for you.
Father, hear the prayers of the family you have gathered here before you.
In mercy and love unite all your children
wherever they may be.*

---

* *In Masses for the Dead the following ending may be used.*

Remember *N.*
In baptism he (she) died with Christ:
may he (she) share his resurrection
when Christ will raise his mortal bodies
and make them like his own in glory.
Welcome into your kingdom our departed
    brothers and sisters,
and all who have left this world in your friendship.
There we hope to share in your glory
when every tear will be wiped away.
On that day we shall see you, our God, as you are.
We shall become like you
and praise you for ever through Christ our Lord,
from whom all good things come.

Welcome into your kingdom our departed brothers and sisters,
and all who have left this world in your friendship.
We hope to enjoy for ever the vision of your glory,
through Christ our Lord, from whom all good things come.

Through him,
with him,
in him,
in the unity of the Holy Spirit,
all glory and honour is yours,
almighty Father,
for ever and ever.
Amen.

*Doxology and
Great Amen*

▶ Continue on p.20

Eucharistic Prayer 4

When this Eucharistic Prayer is used the following Preface is always said.

The Lord be with you.
Lift up your hearts.
Let us give thanks to the Lord our God.

And also with you.
We lift them up to the Lord.
It is right to give him thanks and praise.

Father in heaven,
it is right that we should give you thanks and glory:
you alone are God, living and true.
Through all eternity you live in unapproachable light.
Source of life and goodness, you have created all things,
to fill your creatures with every blessing
and lead all men to the joyful vision of your light.

Countless hosts of angels stand before you to do your will;
they look upon your splendour
and praise you, night and day.

United with them,
and in the name of every creature under heaven,
we too praise your glory as we sing [say]:
Holy, holy, holy Lord ...

Father, we acknowledge your greatness:
all your actions show your wisdom and love.
You formed man in your own likeness
and set him over the whole world
to serve you, his creator,

*Praise of the
Father*

and to rule over all creatures.
Even when he disobeyed you and lost your friendship
you did not abandon him to the power of death,
but helped all men to seek and find you.

Again and again you offered a covenant to man,
and through the prophets taught him to hope for salvation.
Father, you so loved the world
that in the fullness of time you sent your only Son to be our Saviour.
He was conceived through the power of the Holy Spirit,
and born of the Virgin Mary,
a man like us in all things but sin.
To the poor he proclaimed the good news of salvation,
to prisoners, freedom,
and to those in sorrow, joy.
In fulfilment of your will
he gave himself up to death;
but by rising from the dead,
he destroyed death and restored life.
And that we might live no longer for ourselves but for him,
he sent the Holy Spirit from you, Father,
as his first gift to those who believe,
to complete his work on earth
and bring us the fullness of grace.

Father, may the Holy Spirit sanctify these offerings.   *Invocation of*
Let them become the body and blood of Jesus Christ our Lord   *the Spirit*
as we celebrate the great mystery
which he left us as an everlasting covenant.
He always loved those who were his own in the world.
When the time came for him to be glorified by you, his heavenly Father,
he showed the depth of his love.

While they were at supper,   *The Last Supper narrative*
he took bread, said the blessing, broke the bread,   *and Consecration*
and gave it to his disciples, saying:
TAKE THIS, ALL OF YOU, AND EAT IT:
THIS IS MY BODY WHICH WILL BE GIVEN UP FOR YOU.

In the same way, he took the cup, filled with wine.
He gave you thanks, and giving the cup to his disciples, said:
TAKE THIS, ALL OF YOU, AND DRINK FROM IT:
THIS IS THE CUP OF MY BLOOD,
THE BLOOD OF THE NEW AND EVERLASTING COVENANT.
IT WILL BE SHED FOR YOU AND FOR ALL
SO THAT SINS MAY BE FORGIVEN.
DO THIS IN MEMORY OF ME.

The priest (or the deacon, if there is one) says or sings:
Let us proclaim the mystery of faith:

1 **Christ has died,**
   Christ is risen,
   Christ will come again.

3 **When we eat this bread and**
   drink this cup,
   we proclaim your death, Lord Jesus,
   until you come in glory.

Alternative acclamations

2 **Dying you destroyed our death,**
   rising you restored our life.
   Lord Jesus, come in glory.

4 **Lord, by your cross and resurrection**
   you have set us free.
   You are the Saviour of the world.

Father, we now celebrate this memorial of our redemption.
We recall Christ's death, his descent among the dead,
his resurrection, and his ascension to your right hand;
and, looking forward to his coming in glory,
we offer you his body and blood,
the acceptable sacrifice
which brings salvation to the whole world.

Lord, look upon this sacrifice which you have given to your Church;
and by your Holy Spirit, gather all who share this one bread and one cup *
into the one body of Christ, a living sacrifice of praise.   (*ICEL: this bread and wine)

Lord, remember those for whom we offer this sacrifice,   *For the Church,*
especially *N.* our Pope,   *Living and Dead*
N. our bishop, and bishops and clergy everywhere.
Remember those who take part in this offering,
those here present and all your people,
and all who seek you with a sincere heart.
Remember those who have died in the peace of Christ
and all the dead whose faith is known to you alone.
Father, in your mercy grant also to us, your children,
to enter into our heavenly inheritance
in the company of the Virgin Mary, the Mother of God,
and your apostles and saints.
Then, in your kingdom,
freed from the corruption of sin and death,
we shall sing your glory with every creature through Christ our Lord,
through whom you give us everything that is good.

Through him,   *Doxology and*
with him,   *Great Amen*
in him,
in the unity of the Holy Spirit,
all glory and honour is yours,
almighty Father,
for ever and ever.
Amen.

THE COMMUNION RITE

THE LORD'S PRAYER

The priest invites everyone to join in the Lord's Prayer in these or similar words:
Let us pray with confidence to the Father
in the words our Saviour gave us:

Our Father, who art in heaven,
hallowed be thy name.
Thy kingdom come,
thy will be done
on earth as it is in heaven.

Give us this day our daily bread,
and forgive us our trespasses
as we forgive those who trespass against us,
and lead us not into temptation
but deliver us from evil.

Deliver us, Lord, from every evil,
and grant us peace in our day.
In your mercy keep us free from sin
and protect us from all anxiety
as we wait in joyful hope
for the coming of our Saviour, Jesus Christ.
For the kingdom, the power and the glory are yours,
now and for ever.

PRAYER AND SIGN OF PEACE

Lord Jesus Christ, you said to your apostles:
I leave you peace, my peace I give you.
Look not on our sins, but on the faith of your Church,
and grant us the peace and unity of your kingdom
where you live for ever and ever.
Amen.

The peace of the Lord be with you always.
And also with you.

Then the deacon, or the priest, may add:
Let us offer each other the sign of peace.
All make a sign of peace, according to local custom.

THE BREAKING OF BREAD

The priest breaks the hosts in preparation for their distribution at Communion, in accordance with the action of Christ at the Last Supper. He dips a small portion of one of them into the chalice, saying quietly:
May this mingling of the body and blood of our Lord Jesus Christ bring eternal life to us who receive it.

Meanwhile the following is sung or said:
Lamb of God, you take away the sins of the world: have mercy on us.
Lamb of God, you take away the sins of the world: have mercy on us.
Lamb of God, you take away the sins of the world: grant us peace.

PREPARATION FOR COMMUNION

The priest says quietly:

Lord Jesus Christ, Son of the living God, by the will of the Father and the work of the Holy Spirit your death brought life to the world. By your holy body and blood free me from all my sins and from every evil. Keep me faithful to your teaching, and never let me be parted from you. *or*

Lord Jesus Christ, with faith in your love and mercy I eat your body and drink your blood. Let it not bring me condemnation, but health in mind and body.

He continues aloud:

This is the Lamb of God who takes away the sins of the world.
Happy are those who are called to his supper.
Lord, I am not worthy to receive you,
but only say the word and I shall be healed.

THE COMMUNION

Antiphon: ❯ Proper of the Day

During the distribution of Communion a hymn may be sung. If there is no hymn the Communion Antiphon is recited.

As the priest or minister offers the host (and the chalice) to each person he says: The body [or blood] of Christ. *The person receiving Communion replies:* **Amen.**
After communion a period of silence is observed. A thanksgiving hymn may be sung.

PRAYER AFTER COMMUNION

❯ Proper of the Day

To end the Communion Rite the priest reads the Prayer after Communion, in which in the name of the whole assembly he give thanks to God for the great gifts received.

THE CONCLUDING RITE

Brief announcements may be made. Then the priest says:
The Lord be with you. **And also with you.**

BLESSING

The priest blesses the people. On special occasions he may use a solemn blessing.
May almighty God bless you,
the Father, and the Son, and the Holy Spirit.
Amen.

DISMISSAL

The priest dismisses the people with one of the following:
The Mass is ended, go in peace. *or*

Go in the peace of Christ. *or*

Go in peace to love and serve the Lord.
Thanks be to God.

Pentecost Sunday

(The Mass for the Vigil of Pentecost will be found on p.120)

As the priest goes to the altar everyone joins in this Entrance Antiphon or a hymn.

The Spirit of the Lord fills the whole world. It holds all things together and knows every word spoken by man, alleluia.

Turn to page 4

OPENING PRAYER

God our Father,
let the Spirit you sent on your Church
to begin the teaching of the Gospel
continue to work in the world
through the hearts of all who believe.

Father of Light, from whom every good gift comes,
send your Spirit into our lives
with the power of a mighty wind,
and by the flame of your wisdom
open the horizons of our minds.

Loosen our tongues to sing your praise
in words beyond the power of speech,
for without your Spirit
man could never raise his voice in words of peace
or announce the truth that Jesus is Lord,
who lives and reigns with you and the Holy Spirit,
one God, for ever and ever.

FIRST READING   A reading from the Acts of the Apostles
They were all filled with the Holy Spirit and began to speak.   *Acts 2:1-11*

When Pentecost day came round, the apostles had all met in one room, when suddenly they heard what sounded like a powerful wind from heaven, the noise of which filled the entire house in which they were sitting; and something appeared to them that seemed like tongues of fire; these separated and came to rest on the head of each of them. They were all filled with the Holy Spirit, and began to speak foreign languages as the Spirit gave them the gift of speech.

Now there were devout men living in Jerusalem from every nation under heaven, and at this sound they all assembled, each one bewildered to hear these men speaking his own language. They were amazed and astonished. "Surely," they said, "all these men speaking are Galileans? How does it happen that each of us hears them in his own native language? Parthians, Medes and Elamites; people from Mesopotamia, Judaea and Cappadocia, Pontus and Asia, Phrygia and Pamphylia, Egypt and the parts of Libya round Cyrene; as well as visitors from Rome – Jews and proselytes alike – Cretans and Arabs; we hear them preaching in our own language about the marvels of God."

This is the word of the Lord. **Thanks be to God.**

RESPONSORIAL PSALM   *Psalm 103*

Send forth your Spirit, O Lord, and renew the face of the earth. (*or* Alleluia!)

1. Bless the Lord, my soul!
   Lord God, how great you are.
   How many are your works, O Lord!
   The earth is full of your riches.

2. You take back your spirit, they die,
   returning to the dust from which
     they came.
   You send forth your spirit, they are
     created;
   and you renew the face of the earth.

3. May the glory of the Lord last
   forever!
   May the Lord rejoice in his works!
   May my thoughts be pleasing to him.
   I find my joy in the Lord.

SECOND READING   A reading from the first letter of St Paul to the Corinthians
In the one Spirit we were all baptised.   *1 Corinthians 12:3-7,12-13*

No one can say, "Jesus is Lord" unless he is under the influence of the Holy Spirit. There is a variety of gifts but always the same Spirit; there are all sorts of services to be done, but always to the same Lord; working in all sorts of different ways in different people, it is the same God who is working in all of them. The particular way in which the Spirit is given to each person is for a good purpose.
Just as a human body, though it is made of many parts, is a single unit because all these parts, though many, make one body, so it is with Christ. In the one Spirit we were all baptised, Jews as well as Greeks, slaves as well as citizens, and one Spirit was given to us all to drink.
This is the word of the Lord. **Thanks be to God.**

SEQUENCE

1. Holy Spirit, Lord of light,
   from the clear celestial height,
   thy pure beaming radiance give.

2. Come, thou Father of the poor,
   come with treasures which endure,
   come, thou light of all that live!

3. Thou, of all consolers best,
   thou, the soul's delightful guest,
   dost refreshing peace bestow:

4. Thou in toil art comfort sweet;
   pleasant coolness in the heat;
   solace in the midst of woe.

5. Light immortal, light divine,
   visit thou these hearts of thine,
   and our inmost being fill:

6. If thou take thy grace away,
   nothing pure in man will stay;
   all his good is turned to ill.

7. Heal our wounds, our strength
   renew;
   on our dryness pour thy dew;
   wash the stains of guilt away:

8. Bend the stubborn heart and will;
   melt the frozen, warm the chill;
   guide the steps that go astray.

9. Thou, on us who evermore
   thee confess and thee adore,
   with thy sevenfold gifts descend:

10. Give us comfort when we die;
    give us life with thee on high;
    give us joys that never end.

All stand to greet the Gospel. If this Acclamation is not sung it may be omitted.
Alleluia, alleluia! Come, Holy Spirit, fill the hearts of your faithful, and kindle in them the fire of your love. Alleluia!

THE GOSPEL

The Lord be with you. **And also with you.**

A reading from the holy Gospel according to John. **Glory to you, Lord.**

As the Father sent me, so am I sending you: receive the Holy Spirit.

In the evening of the first day of the week, the doors were closed in the room where the disciples were, for fear of the Jews. Jesus came and stood among them. He said to them, "Peace be with you", and showed them his hands and his side. The disciples were filled with joy when they saw the Lord, and he said to them again, "Peace be with you. As the Father sent me, so am I sending you." After saying this he breathed on them and said: "Receive the Holy Spirit. For those whose sins you forgive, they are forgiven; for those whose sins you retain, they are retained."

This is the Gospel of the Lord. **Praise to you, Lord Jesus Christ.**

The Homily follows, then | Turn to page 6 for the Creed |

PRAYER OVER THE GIFTS
Lord,
may the Spirit you promised
lead us into all truth
and reveal to us the full meaning
    of this sacrifice.

PREFACE OF PENTECOST

The Lord be with you.   **And also with you.**

Lift up your hearts.   **We lift them up to the Lord.**

Let us give thanks to the Lord our God.   **It is right to give him thanks and praise.**

Father, all powerful and ever-living God,
we do well always and everywhere to give you thanks.

Today you sent the Holy Spirit
on those marked out to be your children
by sharing the life of your only Son,
and so you brought the paschal mystery to its completion.

Today we celebrate the great beginning of your Church
when the Holy Spirit made known to all peoples the one true God,
and created from the many languages of man
one voice to profess one faith.

The joy of the resurrection renews the whole world,
while the choirs of heaven sing for ever to your glory:

**Holy, holy, holy Lord, God of power and might,
heaven and earth are full of your glory.
Hosanna in the highest.**

**Blessed is he who comes in the name of the Lord.
Hosanna in the highest.**

*Turn to
page 10 for Eucharistic Prayer 1
page 13 for Eucharistic Prayer 2
page 15 for Eucharistic Prayer 3*

COMMUNION ANTIPHON

They were all filled with the Holy Spirit, and they spoke of the great things God had done, alleluia.

PRAYER AFTER COMMUNION
Father,
may the food we receive in the
    eucharist
help our eternal redemption.
Keep within us the vigour of your Spirit
and protect the gifts you have given to
    your Church.

Turn to page 21 for the Concluding Rite

Trinity Sunday

As the priest goes to the altar everyone joins in this Entrance Antiphon or a hymn.

Blessed be God the Father and his only-begotten Son and the Holy Spirit: for he has shown that he loves us.

Turn to page 4

OPENING PRAYER
Father,
you sent your Word to bring us truth
and your Spirit to make us holy.
Through them we come to know
    the mystery of your life.
Help us to worship you, one God
    in three Persons,
by proclaiming and living our faith
    in you.

God, we praise you:
Father all-powerful, Christ Lord and Saviour, Spirit of love.
You reveal yourself in the depths of our being,
drawing us to share in your life and your love.
One God, three Persons, be near to the people formed in your image, close to the world your love brings to life.

FIRST READING   A reading from the book of Exodus

Lord, Lord, a God of tenderness and compassion.   *Exodus 34:4-6, 8-9*

With the two tablets of stone in his hands, Moses went up the mountain of Sinai in the early morning as the Lord had commanded him. And the Lord descended in the form of a cloud, and Moses stood with him there.
He called on the name of the Lord. The Lord passed before him and proclaimed, "Lord, Lord, a God of tenderness and compassion, slow to anger, rich in kindness and faithfulness." And Moses bowed down to the ground at once and worshipped. "If I have indeed won your favour, Lord," he said, "let my Lord come with us, I beg. True, they are a headstrong people, but forgive us our faults and our sins, and adopt us as your heritage."
This is the word of the Lord. **Thanks be to God.**

RESPONSORIAL PSALM   *Daniel 3:52-56*
To you glory and praise for evermore.

1. You are blest, Lord God of our
   fathers.
   To you glory and praise for evermore.
   Blest your glorious holy name.
   To you glory and praise for evermore.

2. You are blest in the temple of your
   glory.
   To you glory and praise for evermore.

3. You are blest on the throne of your
   kingdom.
   To you glory and praise for evermore.

4. You are blest who gaze into the depths.
   To you glory and praise for evermore.

5. You are blessed in the firmament
   of heaven.
   To you glory and praise for evermore.

SECOND READING   A reading from the second letter of
                                           St Paul to the Corinthians

The grace of Jesus Christ, the love of God, and the fellowship of the Holy Spirit.
                                                 2 Corinthians 13:11-13

Brothers, we wish you happiness; try to grow perfect; help one another. Be united;
live in peace, and the God of love and peace will be with you. Greet one another with
the holy kiss. All the saints send you greetings. The grace of the Lord Jesus Christ, the
love of God and the fellowship of the Holy Spirit be with you all.
This is the word of the Lord. **Thanks be to God.**

All stand to greet the Gospel. If this Acclamation is not sung it may be omitted.

**Alleluia, alleluia! Glory be to the Father, and to the Son, and to the Holy Spirit: the
God who is, who was, and who is to come. Alleluia!**

THE GOSPEL   *John 3:16-18*
The Lord be with you. **And also with you.**
A reading from the holy Gospel according to John. **Glory to you, Lord.**

God sent his Son so that through him the world might be saved.

Jesus said to Nicodemus, "God loved the world so much that he gave his only Son, so
that everyone who believes in him may not be lost but may have eternal life. For God
sent his Son into the world not to condemn the world, but so that through him the
world might be saved. No one who believes in him will be condemned; but whoever
refuses to believe is condemned already, because he has refused to believe in the
name of God's only Son."
This is the Gospel of the Lord. **Praise to you, Lord Jesus Christ.**

The Homily follows, then | *Turn to page 6 for the Creed* |

PRAYER OVER THE GIFTS
Lord our God,
make these gifts holy,
and through them
make us a perfect offering to you.

PREFACE OF THE HOLY TRINITY

The Lord be with you.   **And also with you.**
Lift up your hearts.   **We lift them up to the Lord.**
Let us give thanks to the Lord our God.   **It is right to give him thanks and praise.**

Father, all-powerful and ever-living God,
we do well always and everywhere to give you thanks.

We joyfully proclaim our faith
in the mystery of your Godhead.
You have revealed your glory
as the glory also of your Son
and of the Holy Spirit:
three Persons equal in majesty,
undivided in splendour,
yet one Lord, one God,
ever to be adored in your everlasting glory.

And so, with all the choirs of angels in heaven
we proclaim your glory
and join in their unending hymn of praise:

Holy, holy, holy Lord, God of power and might,
heaven and earth are full of your glory.
Hosanna in the highest.

Blessed is he who comes in the name of the Lord.
Hosanna in the highest.

Turn to
page 10 for Eucharistic Prayer 1
page 13 for Eucharistic Prayer 2
page 15 for Eucharistic Prayer 3

COMMUNION ANTIPHON

You are the sons of God, so God has given you the Spirit of his Son to form your hearts and make you cry out: Abba, Father.

PRAYER AFTER COMMUNION

Lord God,
we worship you, a Trinity of Persons,
    one eternal God.
May our faith and the sacrament
    we receive
bring us health of mind and body.

Turn to page 21 for the Concluding Rite

THURSDAY AFTER TRINITY SUNDAY
The Body and Blood of Christ
CORPUS CHRISTI

As the priest goes to the altar everyone joins in this Entrance Antiphon or a hymn.

The Lord fed his people with the finest wheat and honey; their hunger was satisfied.

Turn to page 4

OPENING PRAYER

Lord Jesus Christ,
you gave us the eucharist
as the memorial of your suffering
    and death.
May our worship of this sacrament
of your body and blood help us to
experience the salvation you won for us
and the peace of the kingdom where
you live with the Father and the Holy
    Spirit, one God, for ever and ever.

Lord Jesus Christ,
we worship you living among us
in the sacrament of your body and blood.
May we offer to our father in Heaven
    a solemn pledge of undivided love.
May we offer to our brothers and sisters
a life poured out in loving service of that
kingdom where you live with the Father
and the Holy Spirit, one God, for ever and
ever.

FIRST READING   A reading from the book of Deuteronomy

He fed you with manna which neither you nor your fathers had known.
Deuteronomy 8:2-3,14-16

Moses said to the people: "Remember how the Lord your God led you for forty years
in the wilderness, to humble you, to test you and know your inmost heart – whether
you would keep his commandments or not. He humbled you, he made you feel hunger,
he fed you with manna which neither you nor your fathers had known, to make you
understand that man does not live on bread alone but that man lives on everything that
comes from the mouth of the Lord.
"Do not then forget the Lord your God who brought you out of the land of Egypt, out
of the house of slavery; who guided you through this vast and dreadful wilderness, a
land of fiery serpents, scorpions, thirst; who in this waterless place brought you water
from the hardest rock; who in this wilderness fed you with manna that your fathers
had not known."
This is the word of the Lord. **Thanks be to God.**

RESPONSORIAL PSALM   *Psalm 147*
O praise the Lord, Jerusalem! *or* **Alleluia!**

1. O praise the Lord, Jerusalem!
   Zion, praise your God!
   He has strengthened the bars of your gates,
   he has blessed the children within you.

2. He established peace on your borders,
   he feeds you with finest wheat.
   He sends out his word to the earth
   and swiftly runs his command.

3. He makes his word known to Jacob,
   to Israel his laws and decrees.
   He has not dealt thus with other nations;
   he has not taught them his decrees.

SECOND READING   A reading from the first letter of St Paul to the Corinthians

That there is only one loaf means that, though there are many of us, we form a single body.
1 Corinthians 10:16-17

The blessing-cup that we bless is a communion with the blood of Christ, and the bread that we break is a communion with the body of Christ. The fact that there is only one loaf means that, though there are many of us, we form a single body because we all have a share in this one loaf.
This is the word of the Lord. **Thanks be to God.**

SEQUENCE

Sing forth, O Zion, sweetly sing
The praises of thy Shepherd-King,
In hymns and canticles divine;
Dare all thou canst, thou hast no song
Worthy his praises to prolong,
So far surpassing powers like thine.

Today no theme of common praise
Forms the sweet burden of thy lays-
The living, life-dispensing food-
That food which at the sacred board
Unto the brethren twelve our Lord
His parting legacy bestowed.

Then be the anthem clear and strong,
Thy fullest note, thy sweetest song,
The very music of the breast:
For now shines forth the day sublime
That brings remembrance of time
When Jesus first his table blessed.

Within our new King's banquet-hall
They meet to keep the festival
That closed the ancient paschal rite:
The old is by the new replaced;
The substance hath the shadow chased;
And rising day dispels the night.

Christ willed what he himself had done
Should be renewed while time should run,
In memory of his parting hour:
Thus, tutored in his school divine,
We consecrate the bread and wine;
And lo — a Host of saving power.

This faith to Christian men is given —
Bread is made flesh by words from heaven:
Into his blood the wine is turned:
What though it baffles nature's powers
Of sense and sight? This faith of ours
Proves more than nature e'er discerned.

Concealed beneath the two-fold sign,
Meet symbols of the gifts divine,
There lie the mysteries adored:
The living body is our food;
Our drink the ever-precious blood;
In each, one undivided Lord.

Not he that eateth it divides
The sacred food, which whole abides
Unbroken still, nor knows decay;
Be one, or be a thousand fed,
They eat alike that living bread
Which, still received, ne'er wastes away.

The good, the guilty share therein,
With sure increase of grace or sin,
The ghostly life, or ghostly death:
Death to the guilty; to the good
Immortal life. See how one food
Man's joy or woe accomplisheth.

We break the Sacrament; but bold
And firm thy faith shall keep its hold;
Deem not the whole doth more enfold
Than in the fractured part resides:
Deem not that Christ doth broken lie;
'Tis but the sign that meets the eye;
The hidden deep reality
In all its fullness still abides.

Behold the bread of angels, sent
For pilgrims in their banishment,
The bread for God's true children meant,
That may not unto dogs be given:
Oft in the olden types foreshadowed;
In Isaac on the altar bowed,
And in the ancient paschal food,
And in the manna sent from heaven.

O thou, the wisest, mightiest, best,
Our present food, our future rest,
Come, make us each thy chosen guest,
Co-heirs of thine, and comrades blest
With saints whose dwelling is with thee.

Come then, good shepherd, bread divine,
Still show to us thy mercy sign;
Oh, feed us still, still keep us thine;
So may we see thy glories shine
In fields of immortality;

All stand to greet the Gospel. If this Acclamation is not sung it may be omitted.

Alleluia, alleluia! I am the living bread which has come down from heaven, says the Lord. Anyone who eats this bread will live for ever. Alleluia!

THE GOSPEL   *John 6:51-58*
The Lord be with you. **And also with you.**
A reading from the holy Gospel according to John. **Glory to you, Lord.**

Jesus said to the Jews:
  "I am the living bread which has come down from heaven.
  Anyone who eats this bread will live for ever;
  and the bread that I shall give
  is my flesh, for the life of the world."
  Then the Jews started arguing with one another: "How can this man give us his flesh to eat?" they said. Jesus replied:
  "I tell you most solemnly,
  if you do not eat the flesh of the Son of Man
  and drink his blood,
  you will not have life in you.
  Anyone who does eat my flesh and drink my blood
  has eternal life,
  and I shall raise him up on the last day.
  For my flesh is real food
  and my blood is real drink.
  He who eats my flesh and drinks my blood
  lives in me
  and I live in him.
  As I, who am sent by the living Father,
  myself draw life from the Father,
  so whoever eats me will draw life from me.
  This is the bread come down from heaven:
  not like the bread our ancestors ate:
  they are dead,
  but anyone who eats this bread will live for ever."
This is the Gospel of the Lord. **Praise to you, Lord Jesus Christ.**

The Homily follows, then | *Turn to page 6 for the Creed* |

PRAYER OVER THE GIFTS
Lord,
may the bread and cup we offer
bring your Church the unity and
    peace they signify.

PREFACE OF THE HOLY EUCHARIST I
(The priest may read Preface of the Holy Eucharist II as an alternative)

The Lord be with you.   **And also with you.**
Lift up your hearts.   **We lift them up to the Lord.**
Let us give thanks to the Lord our God.   **It is right to give him thanks and praise.**

Father, all-powerful and ever-living God,
we do well always and everywhere to give you thanks
through Jesus Christ our Lord.

He is the true and eternal priest
who established this unending sacrifice.
He offered himself as a victim for our deliverance
and taught us to make this offering in his memory.
As we eat his body which he gave for us,
we grow in strength.
As we drink his blood which he poured out for us,
we are washed clean.

Now, with angels and archangels,
and the whole company of heaven,
we sing the unending hymn of your praise:

Holy, holy, holy Lord, God of power and might,
heaven and earth are full of your glory.
Hosanna in the highest.

Blessed is he who comes in the name of the Lord.
Hosanna in the highest.

Turn to
page 10 for Eucharistic Prayer 1
page 13 for Eucharistic Prayer 2
page 15 for Eucharistic Prayer 3

COMMUNION ANTIPHON
Whoever eats my flesh and drinks my blood will live in me and I in him, says the Lord.

PRAYER AFTER COMMUNION
Lord Jesus Christ,
you give us your body and blood
    in the eucharist
as a sign that even now we share
    your life.
May we come to possess it completely
    in the kingdom
where you live for ever and ever.

Turn to page 21 for the Concluding Rite

The Sacred Heart of Jesus

As the priest goes to the altar everyone joins in this Entrance Antiphon or a hymn.

The thoughts of his heart last through every generation, that he will rescue them from death and feed them in time of famine.

| Turn to page 4 |

OPENING PRAYER

Father,
we rejoice in the gifts of love
we have received from the heart
   of Jesus your Son.
Open our hearts to share his life
and continue to bless us with his love.

or:
Father,
we have wounded the heart of Jesus
  your Son,
but he brings us forgiveness and grace.
Help us to prove our grateful love
and make amends for our sins.

or:
Let us pray
  (that the love of Christ's heart
  may touch the world with healing
  and peace).

Father,
we honour the heart of your Son
broken by man's cruelty
yet symbol of love's triumph,
pledge of all that man is called to be.

Teach us to see Christ in the lives
  we touch,
to offer him living worship
by love-filled service to our brothers
  and sisters.

FIRST READING   A reading from the book of Deuteronomy
The Lord set his heart on you and chose you.   *Deuteronomy 7:6-11*

Moses said to the people: "You are a people consecrated to the Lord your God; it is you that the Lord our God has chosen to be his very own people out of all the peoples on the earth.
"If the Lord set his heart on you and chose you, it was not because you outnumbered other peoples: you were the least of all peoples. It was for love of you and to keep the oath he swore to your fathers that the Lord brought you out with his mighty hand and redeemed you from the house of slavery, from the power of Pharaoh king of Egypt. Know then that the Lord your God is God indeed, the faithful God who is true to his covenant and his graciousness for a thousand generations towards those who love him and keep his commandments, but who punishes in their own persons those that hate him. He is not slow to destroy the man who hates him; he makes him work out his punishment in person. You are therefore to keep and observe the commandments and statutes and ordinances that I lay down for you today."
This is the word of the Lord. **Thanks be to God.**

RESPONSORIAL PSALM   *Psalm 102*
The love of the Lord is everlasting upon those who hold him in fear.

1. My soul, give thanks to the Lord,
   all my being, bless his holy name.
   My soul, give thanks to the Lord
   and never forget all his blessings.

2. It is he who forgives all your guilt,
   who heals every one of your ills,
   who redeems your life from the grave,
   who crowns you with love
      and compassion.

3. The Lord does deeds of justice,
   gives judgement for all who
      are oppressed.
   He made known his ways to Moses
   and his deeds to Israel's sons.

4. The Lord is compassion and love,
   slow to anger and rich in mercy.
   He does not treat us according
      to our sins
   nor repay us according to our faults.

SECOND READING   A reading from the first letter of St John

Love comes from God.   *1 John 4:7-16*

My dear people,
let us love one another
since love comes from God
and everyone who loves is begotten by God and knows God.
Anyone who fails to love can never have known God,
because God is love.
God's love for us was revealed
when God sent into the world his only Son
so that we could have life through him;
this is the love I mean:
not our love for God,
but God's love for us when he sent his Son
to be the sacrifice that takes our sins away.
My dear people,
since God has loved us so much,
we too should love one another.
No one has ever seen God;
but as long as we love one another
God will live in us
and his love will be complete in us.
We can know that we are living in him
and he is living in us
because he lets us share his Spirit.
We ourselves saw and we testify
that the Father sent his Son
as saviour of the world.
If anyone acknowledges that Jesus is the Son of God,
God lives in him, and he in God.
We ourselves have known and put our faith in God's love towards ourselves.
God is love
and anyone who lives in love lives in God,
and God lives in him.
This is the word of the Lord. **Thanks be to God.**

All stand to greet the Gospel. If this Acclamation is not sung it may be omitted.

Alleluia, alleluia! Shoulder my yoke and learn from me, for I am gentle and humble in heart. Alleluia!

THE GOSPEL   *Matthew 11:25-30*

The Lord be with you. **And also with you.**

A reading from the holy Gospel according to Matthew. **Glory to you, Lord.**

I am gentle and humble in heart.

Jesus exclaimed, "I bless you, Father, Lord of heaven and of earth, for hiding these things from the learned and the clever and revealing them to mere children. Yes, Father, for that is what it pleased you to do. Everything has been entrusted to me by my Father; and no one knows the Son except the Father, just as no one knows the Father except the Son and those to whom the Son chooses to reveal him.

Come to me, all you who labour and are overburdened and I will give you rest. Shoulder my yoke and learn from me, for I am gentle and humble in heart, and you will find rest for your souls. Yes, my yoke is easy and my burden light."

This is the Gospel of the Lord. **Praise to you, Lord Jesus Christ.**

The Homily follows, then Turn to page 6 for the Creed

PRAYER OVER THE GIFTS

Lord,
look on the heart of Christ your Son
filled with love for us.
Because of his love
accept our eucharist and forgive our sins.

PREFACE OF THE SACRED HEART

The Lord be with you.   **And also with you.**

Lift up your hearts.   **We lift them up to the Lord.**

Let us give thanks to the Lord our God.   **It is right to give him thanks and praise.**

Father, all-powerful and ever-living God,
we do well always and everywhere to give you thanks
through Jesus Christ our Lord.

Lifted high on the cross,
Christ gave his life for us,
so much did he love us.
From his wounded side flowed blood and water,
the fountain of sacramental life in the Church.
To his open heart the Saviour invites all men,
to draw water in joy from the springs of salvation.

Now, with all the saints and angels,
we praise you for ever:

**Holy, holy, holy Lord, God of power and might,
heaven and earth are full of your glory.
    Hosanna in the highest.
Blessed is he who comes in the name of the Lord.
    Hosanna in the highest.**

*Turn to
page 10 for Eucharistic Prayer 1
page 13 for Eucharistic Prayer 2
page 15 for Eucharistic Prayer 3*

COMMUNION ANTIPHON

The Lord says: If anyone is thirsty, let him come to me; whoever believes in me, let him drink. Streams of living water shall flow out from within him.

One of the soldiers pierced Jesus' side with a lance, and at once there flowed out blood and water.

PRAYER AFTER COMMUNION
Father,
may this sacrament fill us with love.
Draw us closer to Christ your Son
and help us to recognise him in others.

Turn to page 21 for the Concluding Rite

7th Sunday in Ordinary Time

As the priest goes to the altar everyone joins in this Entrance Antiphon or a hymn.

Lord, your mercy is my hope, my heart rejoices in your saving power. I will sing to the Lord for his goodness to me.

Turn to page 4

OPENING PRAYER

Father,
keep before us the wisdom and love
you have revealed in your Son.
Help us to be like him
in word and deed,
for he lives and reigns with you and the
    Holy Spirit,
one God, for ever and ever.

Almighty God,
Father of our Lord Jesus Christ,
faith in your word is the way to
    wisdom,
and to ponder your divine plan is to
    grow in the truth.

Open our eyes to your deeds,
our ears to the sound of your call,
so that our every act may increase our
    sharing
in the life you have offered us.

FIRST READING   A reading from the book of Leviticus
You must love your neighbour as yourself   *Leviticus 19:1-2, 17-18*

The Lord spoke to Moses; he said: "Speak to the whole community of the sons of Israel and say to them: 'Be holy, for I, the Lord your God, am holy'.

'You must not bear hatred for your brother in your heart. You must openly tell him, your neighbour, of this offence: this way you will not take a sin upon yourself. You must not exact vengeance, nor must you bear a grudge against the children of your people. You must love your neighbour as yourself. I am the Lord.'"

This is the word of the Lord. **Thanks be to God.**

RESPONSORIAL PSALM   *Psalm 102*

The Lord is compassion and love.

1. My soul, give thanks to the Lord,
   all my being, bless his holy name.
   My soul, give thanks to the Lord
   and never forget all his blessings.

2. It is he who forgives all your guilt,
   who heals every one of your ills,
   who redeems your life from the grave,
   who crowns you with love and
   compassion.

3. The Lord is compassion and love,
   slow to anger and rich in mercy.
   He does not treat us according to our
   sins
   nor repay us according to our faults.

4. As far as the east is from the west
   so far does he remove our sins.
   As a father has compassion on his sons,
   the Lord has pity on those who fear him.

SECOND READING   A reading from the first letter of St Paul to the Corinthians

All are your servants, but you belong to Christ and Christ belongs to God.

1 Corinthians 3:16-23

Didn't you realise that you were God's temple and that the Spirit of God was living
among you? If anybody should destroy the temple of God, God will destroy him,
because the temple of God is sacred: and you are that temple.

Make no mistake about it: if any one of you think of himself as wise, in the ordinary
sense of the word, then he must learn to be a fool before he really can be wise. Why?
Because the wisdom of this world is foolishness to God. As scripture says: The Lord
knows wise men's thoughts: he knows how useless they are, or again: God is not
convinced by the arguments of the wise. So there is nothing to boast about in anything
human: Paul, Apollos, Cephas, the world, life and death, the present and the future,
are all your servants; but you belong to Christ and Christ belongs to God.

This is the word of the Lord. **Thanks be to God.**

All stand to greet the Gospel. If this Acclamation is not sung it may be omitted.

**Alleluia, alleluia! If anyone loves me he will keep my word, and my Father will
love him, and we shall come to him. Alleluia!**
or:
**Alleluia, alleluia! When anyone obeys what Christ has said, God's love comes to
perfection in him. Alleluia!**

THE GOSPEL   *Matthew 5:38-48*

The Lord be with you. **And also with you.**

A reading from the holy Gospel according to Matthew. **Glory to you, Lord.**

Love your enemies.

Jesus said to his disciples: "You have learnt how it was said: Eye for eye and tooth for
tooth. But I say this to you: offer the wicked man no resistance. On the contrary, if
anyone hits you on the right cheek, offer him the other as well; if a man takes you to
law and would have your tunic let him have your cloak as well. And if anyone orders
you to go one mile, go two miles with him. Give to anyone who asks, and if anyone
wants to borrow, do not turn away.

"You have learnt how it was said: You must love your neighbour and hate your
enemy. But I say this to you: love your enemies and pray for those who persecute you;
in this way you will be sons of your Father in heaven, for he causes his sun to rise on

bad men as well as good and his rain to fall on honest and dishonest men alike. For if you love those who love you, what right have you to claim any credit? Even the tax collectors do as much, do they not? And if you save your greetings for your brothers, are you doing anything exceptional? Even the pagans do as much, do they not? You must therefore be perfect just as your heavenly Father is perfect."
     This is the Gospel of the Lord. **Praise to you Lord Jesus Christ.**

The Homily follows, then   Turn to page 6 for the Creed

PRAYER OVER THE GIFTS

Lord,
as we make this offering,
may our worship in Spirit and truth
bring us salvation.

Turn to page 9 for the Sunday Prefaces

COMMUNION ANTIPHON

I will tell all your marvellous works. I will rejoice and be glad in you, and sing to your name, Most High.

Lord, I believe that you are Christ, the Son of God, who was to come into this world.

PRAYER AFTER COMMUNION

Almighty God,
help us to live the example of love
we celebrate in this eucharist,
that we may come to its fulfilment in your presence.

Turn to page 21 for the Concluding Rite

8th Sunday in Ordinary Time

As the priest goes to the altar everyone joins in this Entrance Antiphon or hymn.

The Lord has been my strength; he has led me into freedom. He saved me because he loves me.

Turn to page 4

OPENING PRAYER

Lord,
guide the course of world events
and give your Church the joy and peace
of serving you in freedom.

Father in heaven,
form in us the likeness of your Son
and deepen his life within us.
Send us as witnesses of gospel joy
into a world of fragile peace and broken
     promises.
Touch the hearts of all men with your
     love
that they in turn may love one another.

FIRST READING   A reading from the prophet Isaiah

I will never forget you.   *Isaiah 49:14-15*

Zion was saying, "The Lord has abandoned me, the Lord has forgotten me." Does a woman forget her baby at the breast, or fail to cherish the son of her womb? Yet even if these forget, I will never forget you.

This is the word of the Lord. **Thanks be to God.**

RESPONSORIAL PSALM   *Psalm 61*

In God alone is my soul at rest.

1. In God alone is my soul at rest;
   my help comes from him.
   He alone is my rock, my stronghold,
   my fortress: I stand firm.

2. In God alone be at rest, my soul;
   for my hope comes from him.
   He alone is my rock, my stronghold
   my fortress: I stand firm.

3. In God is my safety and glory,
   the rock of my strength.
   Take refuge in God all you people.
   Trust him at all times.
   Pour out your hearts before him.

SECOND READING   A reading from the first letter of St Paul to the Corinthians

The Lord will reveal the secret intentions of men's hearts.   *1 Corinthians 4:1-5*

People must think of us as Christ's servants, stewards entrusted with the mysteries of God. What is expected of stewards is that each one should be found worthy of his trust. Not that it makes the slightest difference to me whether you, or indeed any human tribunal, find me worthy or not. I will not even pass judgement on myself. True, my conscience does not reproach me at all, but that does not prove that I am acquitted: the Lord alone is my judge. There must be no passing of premature judgement. Leave that until the Lord comes: he will light up all that is hidden in the dark and reveal the secret intentions of men's hearts. Then will be the time for each one to have whatever praise he deserves, from God.

This is the word of the Lord. **Thanks be to God.**

All stand to greet the Gospel. If this Acclamation is not sung it may be omitted.

Alleluia, alleluia! Your word is truth, O Lord, consecrate us in the truth. Alleluia!
or
Alleluia, alleluia! The word of God is something alive and active: it can judge secret emotions and thoughts. Alleluia!

THE GOSPEL   *Matthew 6:24-34*

The Lord be with you. **And also with you.**

A reading from the holy Gospel according to Matthew. **Glory to you, Lord.**

Do not worry about tomorrow.

Jesus said to his disciples: "No one can be the slave of two masters: he will either hate the first and love the second, or treat the first with respect and the second with scorn. You cannot be the slave both of God and of money. That is why I am telling you not to worry about your life and what you are to eat, nor about your body and how you are to clothe it. Surely life means more than food, and the body more than clothing! Look at the birds in the sky. They do not sow or reap or gather into barns; yet your heavenly Father feeds them. Are you not worth much more than they are? Can any of you, for all his worrying, add one single cubit to his span of life? And why worry about clothing? Think of the flowers growing in the fields; they never have to work or spin; yet I assure you that not even Solomon in all his regalia was robed like one of these. Now if that is how God clothes the grass in the field which is there today and thrown into the furnace tomorrow, will he not much more look after you, you men of little faith? So do not worry; do not say, 'What are we to eat? What are we to drink? How are we to be clothed?' It is the pagans who set their hearts on all these things. Your heavenly Father knows you need them all. Set your hearts on his kingdom first, and on his righteousness, and all these other things will be given to you as well. So do not worry about tomorrow: tomorrow will take care of itself. Each day has enough trouble of its own".

This is the Gospel of the Lord. **Praise to you, Lord Jesus Christ.**

The Homily follows, then *Turn to page 6 for the Creed*

PRAYER OVER THE GIFTS

God our Creator,
may this bread and wine we offer
as a sign of our love and worship
lead us to salvation.

Turn to page 9 for the Sunday Prefaces

COMMUNION ANTIPHON

I will sing to the Lord for his goodness to me, I will sing the name of the Lord, Most High.

I, the Lord, am with you always, until the end of the world.

PRAYER AFTER COMMUNION

God of salvation,
may this sacrament which strengthens us here on earth
bring us to eternal life.

Turn to page 21 for the Concluding Rite.

9th Sunday in Ordinary Time

As the priest goes to the altar everyone joins in this Entrance Antiphon or a hymn.

O look at me and be merciful, for I am wretched and alone. See my hardship and my poverty, and pardon all my sins.

Turn to page 4

OPENING PRAYER

Father,
your love never fails.
Hear our call.
Keep us from danger
and provide for all our needs.

God our Father,
teach us to cherish the gifts that surround us.
Increase our faith in you
and bring our trust to its promised fulfilment
in the joy of your kingdom.

FIRST READING

A reading from the book of Deuteronomy

See, I set before you today a blessing and a curse.   *Deuteronomy 11:18,26-28,32*

Moses said to the people: "Let these words of mine remain in your heart and in your soul; fasten them on your hand as a sign and on your forehead as a circlet.
"See, I set before you today a blessing and a curse: a blessing, if you obey the commandments of the Lord our God that I enjoin on you today; a curse, if you disobey the commandments of the Lord your God and leave the way I have marked out for you today, by going after other gods you have not known. You must keep and observe all the laws and customs that I set before you today."
This is the word of the Lord. **Thanks be to God.**

RESPONSORIAL PSALM

Psalm 30

Be a rock of refuge for me, O Lord.

1. In you, O Lord, I take refuge.
   Let me never be put to shame.
   In your justice, set me free,
   hear me and speedily rescue me.

2. Be a rock of refuge for me,
   a mighty stronghold to save me,
   for you are my rock, my stronghold.
   For your name's sake, lead me and
   guide me.

3. Let your face shine on your servant.
   Save me in your love.
   Be strong, let your heart take courage,
   all who hope in the Lord.

SECOND READING

A reading from the letter of St Paul to the Romans

A man is justified by faith and not by doing something the Law tells him to do.
Romans 3:21-25,28

God's justice that was made known through the Law and the Prophets has now been revealed outside the Law, since it is the same justice of God that comes through faith to everyone, Jew and pagan alike, who believes in Jesus Christ. Both Jew and pagan sinned and forfeited God's glory, and both are justified through the free gift of his grace by being redeemed in Christ Jesus who was appointed by God to sacrifice his

life so as to win reconciliation through faith since, as we see it, a man is justified by faith and not by doing something the Law tells him to do.
This is the word of the Lord. **Thanks be to God.**

All stand to greet the Gospel. If this Acclamation is not sung it may be omitted.
Alleluia, alleluia! If anyone loves me he will keep my word, and my Father will love him, and we shall come to him. Alleluia!

or **Alleluia, alleluia! I am the vine, you are the branches, says the Lord. Whoever remains in me, with me in him, bears fruit in plenty. Alleluia!**

THE GOSPEL   *Matthew 7:21-27*
The Lord be with you. **And also with you.**
A reading from the holy Gospel according to Matthew. **Glory to you, Lord.**
The house built on rock and the house built on sand.

Jesus said to his disciples: "It is not those who say to me, 'Lord, Lord', who will enter the kingdom of heaven, but the person who does the will of my father in heaven. When the day comes many will say to me, 'Lord, Lord, did we not prophesy in your name, cast out demons in your name, work many miracles in your name?' Then I shall tell them to their faces: I have never known you; away from me, you evil men!
"Therefore, everyone who listens to these words of mine and acts on them will be like a sensible man who built his house on rock. Rain came down, floods rose, gales blew and hurled themselves against that house, and it did not fall: it was founded on rock. But everyone who listens to these words of mine and does not act on them will be like a stupid man who built his house on sand. Rain came down, floods rose, gales blew and struck that house, and it fell; and what a fall it had!"
This is the Gospel of the Lord. **Praise to you, Lord Jesus Christ.**

The Homily follows, then | *Turn to page 6 for the Creed* |

PRAYER OVER THE GIFTS
Lord,
as we gather to offer our gifts
confident in your love,
make us holy by sharing your life with
us and by this eucharist forgive our sins.

| *Turn to pages 8-10 for the Preface and Eucharistic Prayer* |

COMMUNION ANTIPHON
I call upon you, God, for you will answer me; bend your ear and hear my prayer.

I tell you solemnly, whatever you ask for in prayer, believe that you have received it, and it will be yours, says the Lord.

PRAYER AFTER COMMUNION
Lord,
as you give us the body and blood
  of your Son,
guide us with your Spirit
that we may honour you
not only with our lips,
but also with the lives we lead,
and so enter your kingdom.

Turn to page 21 for the Concluding Rite

10th Sunday in Ordinary Time

As the priest goes to the altar everyone joins in this Entrance Antiphon or a hymn.

The Lord is my light and my salvation. Who shall frighten me? The Lord is the defender of my life. Who shall make me tremble?

Turn to page 4

OPENING PRAYER
God of wisdom and love,
source of all good,
send your Spirit to teach us your truth
and guide our actions
in your way of peace.

Father in heaven,
words cannot measure the boundaries of love
for those born to new life in Christ Jesus.
Raise us beyond the limits this world imposes,
so that we may be free to love as Christ teaches
and find our joy in your glory.

FIRST READING   A reading from the prophet Hosea

What I want is love, not sacrifice.   *Hosea 6:3-6*

Let us set ourselves to know the Lord; that he will come is as certain as the dawn. His judgement will rise like the light, he will come to us as showers come, like spring rains watering the earth.
What am I to do with you, Ephraim? What am I to do with you, Judah? This love of yours is like a morning cloud, like the dew that quickly disappears. This is why I have torn them to pieces by the prophets, why I slaughtered them with the words from my mouth, since what I want is love, not sacrifice; knowledge of God, not holocausts.
This is the word of the Lord. **Thanks be to God.**

RESPONSORIAL PSALM   *Psalm 49*
I will show God's salvation to the upright.

1. The God of gods, the Lord,
   has spoken and summoned the earth,
   from the rising of the sun to its setting,
   "I find no fault with your sacrifices,
   your offerings are always before me."

2. "Were I hungry, I would not tell you,
   for I own the world and all it holds.
   Do you think I eat the flesh of bulls,
   or drink the blood of goats?"

3. "Pay your sacrifice of thanksgiving to God
   and render him your votive offerings.
   Call on me in the day of distress.
   I will free you and you shall honour me."

SECOND READING   A reading from the letter of St Paul to the Romans

Abraham drew strength from faith and gave glory to God.   *Romans 4:18-25*

Though it seemed Abraham's hope could not be fulfilled, he hoped and he believed, and through doing so he did become the father of many nations exactly as he had been promised: Your descendants will be as many as the stars. Even the thought that his body was past fatherhood – he was about a hundred years old – and Sarah too old to become a mother, did not shake his belief. Since God had promised it, Abraham refused either to deny it or even to doubt it, but drew strength from faith and gave glory to God, convinced that God had power to do what he had promised. This is the faith that was "considered as justifying him". Scripture however does not refer only to him but to us as well when it says that his faith was thus "considered"; our faith too will be "considered" if we believe in him who raised Jesus our Lord from the dead, Jesus who was put to death for our sins and raised to life to justify us.
This is the word of the Lord. **Thanks be to God.**

All stand to greet the Gospel. If this Acclamation is not sung it may be omitted.
Alleluia, alleluia! Open our heart, O Lord, to accept the words of your Son. Alleluia!
or **Alleluia, alleluia! The Lord has sent me to bring the good news to the poor, to proclaim liberty to captives. Alleluia!**

GOSPEL   *Matthew 9:9-13*
The Lord be with you. **And also with you.**
A reading from the holy Gospel according to Matthew. **Glory to you, Lord.**

I did not come to call the virtuous, but sinners.

As Jesus was walking on he saw a man named Matthew sitting by the customs house, and he said to him, "Follow me." And he got up and followed him.
While he was at dinner in the house it happened that a number of tax collectors and sinners came to sit at the table with Jesus and his disciples. When the Pharisees saw this, they said to the disciples, "Why does your master eat with tax collectors and sinners?" When he heard this he replied, "It is not the healthy who need the doctor, but the sick. Go and learn the meaning of the words: What I want is mercy, not sacrifice. And indeed I did not come to call the virtuous, but sinners."
This is the Gospel of the Lord. **Praise to you, Lord Jesus Christ.**

The Homily follows, then Turn to page 6 for the Creed

PRAYER OVER THE GIFTS
Lord,
look with love on our service.
Accept the gifts we bring
and help us grow in Christian love.

Turn to pages 8-10 for the Preface and Eucharistic Prayer

COMMUNION ANTIPHON
I can rely on the Lord; I can always turn to him for shelter. It was he who gave me my freedom. My God, you are always there to help me!

God is love, and he who lives in love, lives in God, and God in him.

PRAYER AFTER COMMUNION
Lord,
may your healing love
turn us from sin
and keep us on the way that leads to you.

Turn to page 21 for the Concluding Rite

11th Sunday in Ordinary Time

As the priest goes to the altar everyone joins in this Entrance Antiphon or a hymn.

Lord, hear my voice when I call to you. You are my help; do not cast me off, do not desert me, my Saviour God.

Turn to page 4

OPENING PRAYER
Almighty God,
our hope and our strength,
without you we falter.
Help us to follow Christ
and to live according to your will.

God our Father,
we rejoice in the faith that draws us together,
aware that selfishness can drive us apart.
Let your encouragement be our constant strength.
Keep us one in the love that has sealed our lives,
help us to live as one family
the gospel we profess.

FIRST READING   A reading from the book of Exodus
I will count you a kingdom of priests, a consecrated nation.   *Exodus 19:2-6*

From Rephidim the Israelites set out again; and when they reached the wilderness of Sinai, there in the wilderness they pitched their camp; there facing the mountain Israel pitched camp.
Moses then went up to God, and the Lord called to him from the mountain, saying, "Say this to the House of Jacob, declare this to the sons of Israel, 'You yourselves have seen what I did with the Egyptians, how I carried you on eagle's wings and brought you to myself. From this you know that now, if you obey my voice and hold fast to my covenant, you of all the nations shall be my very own for all the earth is mine. I will count you a kingdom of priests, a consecrated nation.' "
This is the word of the Lord. **Thanks be to God.**

RESPONSORIAL PSALM   *Psalm 99*
We are his people, the sheep of his flock.

1. Cry out with joy to the Lord,
   all the earth.
   Serve the Lord with gladness.
   Come before him, singing for joy.

2. Know that he, the Lord, is God.
   He made us, we belong to him,
   we are his people, the sheep of his flock.

3. Indeed, how good is the Lord,
   eternal his merciful love.
   He is faithful from age to age.

SECOND READING   A reading from the letter of St Paul to the Romans
Now that we have been reconciled by the death of his Son, surely we may count on being saved by the life of his Son.   *Romans 5:6-11*

We were still helpless when at his appointed moment Christ died for sinful men. It is not easy to die even for a good man – though of course for someone really worthy, a man might be prepared to die – but what proves that God loves us is that Christ died for us while we were still sinners. Having died to make us righteous, is it likely that he would now fail to save us from God's anger? When we were reconciled to God by the death of his Son, we were still enemies; now that we have been reconciled, surely we may count on being saved by the life of his Son? Not merely because we have been reconciled but because we are filled with joyful trust in God, through our Lord Jesus Christ, through whom we have already gained our reconciliation.
This is the word of the Lord. **Thanks be to God.**

All stand to greet the Gospel. If this Acclamation is not sung it may be omitted.
Alleluia, alleluia! The sheep that belong to me listen to my voice, says the Lord, I know them and they follow me. Alleluia!
or **Alleluia, alleluia! The kingdom of God is close at hand. Repent, and believe the Good News. Alleluia!**

GOSPEL   *Matthew: 9:36-10:8*
The Lord be with you. **And also with you.**
A reading from the holy Gospel according to Matthew. **Glory to you, Lord**.

He summoned his twelve disciples and sent them out.

When Jesus saw the crowds he felt sorry for them because they were harassed and dejected, like sheep without a shepherd. Then he said to his disciples, "The harvest is rich but the labourers are few, so ask the Lord of the harvest to send labourers to his harvest."
He summoned his twelve disciples, and gave them authority over unclean spirits with power to cast them out and to cure all kinds of diseases and sickness.
These are the names of the twelve apostles: first, Simon who is called Peter, and his brother Andrew; James the son of Zebedee, and his brother John; Philip and Bartholomew; Thomas, and Matthew the tax collector; James the son of Alphaeus, and Thaddaeus; Simon the Zealot and Judas Iscariot, the one who was to betray him. These twelve Jesus sent out, instructing them as follows:
"Do not turn your steps to pagan territory, and do not enter any Samaritan town; go rather to the lost sheep of the House of Israel. And as you go, proclaim that the kingdom

of heaven is close at hand. Cure the sick, raise the dead, cleanse the lepers, cast out devils. You received without charge, give without charge."
This is the Gospel of the Lord. **Praise to you, Lord Jesus Christ.**

The Homily follows, then   Turn to page 6 for the Creed

PRAYER OVER THE GIFTS
Lord God,
in this bread and wine
you give us food for body and spirit.
May the eucharist renew our strength   *Turn to pages 8-10 for the Preface and*
and bring us health of mind and body.   *Eucharistic Prayer*

COMMUNION ANTIPHON
One thing I seek: to dwell in the house of   **Father, keep in your name those you have**
the Lord all the days of my life.   **given me, that they may be one as we are**
    one, says the Lord.

PRAYER AFTER COMMUNION
Lord,
may this eucharist
accomplish in your Church   *Turn to page 21 for the Concluding Rite*
the unity and peace it signifies.

12th Sunday in Ordinary Time

As the priest goes to the altar everyone joins in this Entrance Antiphon or a hymn.
God is the strength of his people. In him, we his chosen live in safety. Save us, Lord,
who share in your life, and give us your blessing; be our shepherd for ever.

Turn to page 4

OPENING PRAYER
Father,   God of the universe,
guide and protector of your people,   we worship you as Lord.
grant us an unfailing respect for your   God, ever close to us,
name, and keep us always in your love.   we rejoice to call you Father.
    From this world's uncertainty we look
    to your covenant.
    Keep us one in your peace, secure in
    your love.

FIRST READING   A reading from the prophet Jeremiah
He has delivered the soul of the needy from the hands of evil men.   *Jeremiah 20:10-13*

Jeremiah said: "I hear so many disparaging me, 'Terror from every side! Denounce him! Let us denounce him!' All those who used to be my friends watched for my downfall, 'Perhaps he will be seduced into error. Then we will master him and take

our revenge!' But the Lord is at my side, a mighty hero; my opponents will stumble, mastered, confounded by their failure; everlasting, unforgettable disgrace will be theirs. But you, Lord of Hosts, you who probe with justice, who scrutinise the loins and heart, let me see the vengeance you will take on them, for I have committed my cause to you. Sing to the Lord, praise the Lord, for he has delivered the soul of the needy from the hands of evil men."
This is the word of the Lord. **Thanks be to God.**

RESPONSORIAL PSALM   *Psalm 68*
In your great love, answer me, O God.

1. It is for you that I suffer taunts,
     that shame covers my face,
     that I have become a stranger to
        my brothers,
     an alien to my own mother's sons.
   I burn with zeal for your house
   and taunts against you fall on me.

2. This is my prayer to you,
     my prayer for your favour.
   In your great love, answer me, O God,
     with your help that never fails:
   Lord, answer, for your love is kind;
     in your compassion, turn towards me.

3. The poor when they see it will be glad
     and God-seeking hearts will revive;
   for the Lord listens to the needy
     and does not spurn his servants in their chains.
   Let the heavens and the earth give him praise,
     the sea and all its living creatures.

SECOND READING   A reading from the letter of St Paul to the Romans

The gift considerably outweighed the fall.   *Romans 5:12-15*

Sin entered the world through one man, and through sin death, and thus death has spread through the whole human race because everyone has sinned. Sin existed in the world long before the Law was given. There was no law and so no one could be accused of the sin of 'law-breaking', yet death reigned over all from Adam to Moses, even though their sin, unlike that of Adam, was not a matter of breaking a law.
Adam prefigured the One to come, but the gift itself considerably outweighed the fall. If it is certain that through one man's fall so many died, it is even more certain that divine grace, coming through the one man, Jesus Christ, came to so many as an abundant free gift.
This is the word of the Lord. **Thanks be to God.**

All stand to greet the Gospel. If this Acclamation is not sung it may be omitted.
Alleluia, alleluia! The Word was made flesh and lived among us; to all who did accept him he gave power to become children of God. Alleluia!

or **Alleluia, alleluia! The Spirit of truth will be my witness; and you too will be my witnesses. Alleluia!**

GOSPEL   *Matthew 10:26-33*
The Lord be with you. **And also with you.**
A reading from the holy Gospel according to Matthew. **Glory to you, Lord.**

Do not be afraid of those who kill the body.

Jesus instructed the Twelve as follows: "Do not be afraid. For everything that is now covered will be uncovered, and everything now hidden will be made clear. What I say to you in the dark, tell in the daylight; what you hear in whispers, proclaim from the housetops.

"Do not be afraid of those who kill the body but cannot kill the soul; fear him rather who can destroy both body and soul in hell. Can you not buy two sparrows for a penny? And yet not one falls to the ground without your Father knowing. Why, every hair on your head has been counted. So there is no need to be afraid; you are worth more than hundreds of sparrows.

"So if anyone declares himself for me in the presence of men, I will declare myself for him in the presence of my Father in heaven. But the one who disowns me in the presence of men, I will disown in the presence of my Father in heaven."
This is the Gospel of the Lord. **Praise to you, Lord Jesus Christ.**

The Homily follows, then | *Turn to page 6 for the Creed* |

PRAYER OVER THE GIFTS
Lord,
receive our offering,
and may this sacrifice of praise
purify us in mind and heart
and make us always eager to serve you.

| *Turn to pages 8-10 for the Preface and Eucharistic Prayer* |

COMMUNION ANTIPHON
The eyes of all look to you, O Lord, and you give them food in due season.   **I am the Good Shepherd; I give my life for my sheep, says the Lord.**

PRAYER AFTER COMMUNION
Lord,
you give us the body and blood
    of your Son
to renew your life within us.
In your mercy, assure our redemption
and bring us to the eternal life
we celebrate in this eucharist .

| *Turn to page 21 for the Concluding Rite* |

13th Sunday in Ordinary Time

As the priest goes to the altar everyone joins in this Entrance Antiphon or a hymn.

All nations, clap your hands. Shout with a voice of joy to God. | *Turn to page 4* |

OPENING PRAYER

Father,
you call your children
to walk in the light of Christ.
Free us from darkness
and keep us in the radiance
   of your truth.

Father in heaven,
the light of Jesus
has scattered the darkness of hatred and
sin.
Called to that light
we ask for your guidance.
Form our lives in your truth, our hearts
in your love.

FIRST READING · A reading from the second book of Kings
This is a holy man of God; let him rest there. · *2 Kings 4:8-11,14-16*

One day as Elisha was on his way to Shunem, a woman of rank who lived there pressed him to stay and eat there. After this he always broke journey for a meal when he passed that way. She said to her husband, "Look I am sure the man who is constantly passing our way must be a holy man of God. Let us build him a small room on the roof, and put him a bed in it, and a table and chair and lamp; whenever he comes to us he can rest there." One day when he came, he retired to the upper room and lay down. "What can be done for her?" he asked. Gehazi answered, "Well, she has no son and her husband is old." Elisha said, "Call her." The servant called her and she stood at the door. "This time next year," he said, "you will hold a son in your arms." This is the word of the Lord. **Thanks be to God.**

RESPONSORIAL PSALM · *Psalm 88*
I will sing for ever of your love, O Lord.

1. I will sing for ever of your love, O Lord;
   through all ages my mouth will proclaim your truth.
   Of this I am sure, that your love lasts for ever,
   that your truth is firmly established as the heavens.

2. Happy the people who acclaim such a king,
   who walk, O Lord, in the light of your face,
   who find their joy every day in your name,
   who make your justice the source of their bliss.

3. For it is you, O Lord, who are the glory of their strength;
   it is by your favour that our might is exalted:
   for our ruler is in the keeping of the Lord;
   our king is in the keeping of the Holy One of Israel.

SECOND READING · A reading from the letter of St Paul to the Romans
When we were baptised we went into the tomb with Christ, so that we too might live a new life. · *Romans 6:3-4,8-11*

When we were baptised in Christ Jesus we were baptised in his death; in other words, when we were baptised we went into the tomb with him and joined him in death, so that as Christ was raised from the dead by the Father's glory, we too might live a new life.

But we believe that having died with Christ we shall return to life with him: Christ, as we know, having been raised from the dead will never die again. Death has no power over him any more. When he died, he died, once for all, to sin, so his life now is life with God; and in that way, you too must consider yourselves to be dead to sin but alive for God in Christ Jesus.

This is the word of the Lord. **Thanks be to God.**

All stand to greet the Gospel. If this Acclamation is not sung it may be omitted.
Alleluia, alleluia! Open our heart, O Lord, to accept the words of your Son. Alleluia!

or **Alleluia, alleluia! You are a chosen race, a royal priesthood, a people set apart to sing the praises of God who called you out of darkness into his wonderful light. Alleluia!**

GOSPEL   *Matthew 10:37-42*
The Lord be with you. **And also with you.**
A reading from the holy Gospel according to Matthew. **Glory to you, Lord.**

Anyone who does not take his cross is not worthy of me. Anyone who welcomes you welcomes me.

Jesus instructed the Twelve as follows: "Anyone who prefers father or mother to me is not worthy of me. Anyone who prefers son or daughter to me is not worthy of me. Anyone who does not take his cross and follow in my footsteps is not worthy of me. Anyone who finds his life will lose it; anyone who loses his life for my sake will find it. Anyone who welcomes you welcomes me; and those who welcome me welcome the one who sent me.

"Anyone who welcomes a prophet because he is a prophet will have a prophet's reward; and anyone who welcomes a holy man because he is a holy man will have a holy man's reward.

"If anyone gives so much as a cup of cold water to one of these little ones because he is a disciple, then I tell you solemnly, he will most certainly not lose his reward."
This is the Gospel of the Lord. **Praise to you, Lord Jesus Christ.**

The Homily follows, then   Turn to page 6 for the Creed

PRAYER OVER THE GIFTS
Lord God,
through your sacraments
you give us the power of your grace.
May this eucharist   *Turn to pages 8-10 for the Preface and Eucharistic Prayer*
help us to serve you faithfully.

COMMUNION ANTIPHON
O, bless the Lord, my soul, and all that is within me bless his holy name.   **Father, I pray for them: may they be one in us, so that the world may believe it was you who sent me.**

PRAYER AFTER COMMUNION
Lord,
may this sacrifice and communion
give us a share in your life
and help us bring your love to the world.

Turn to page 21 for the Concluding Rite

14th Sunday in Ordinary Time

As the priest goes to the altar everyone joins in this Entrance Antiphon or a hymn.

Within your temple, we ponder your loving kindness, O God. As your name, so also your praise reaches to the ends of the earth; your right hand is filled with justice.

Turn to page 4

OPENING PRAYER

Father,
through the obedience of Jesus,
your servant and your Son,
you raised a fallen world.
Free us from sin
and bring us the joy that lasts for ever.

Father,
in the rising of your Son
death gives birth to new life.
The sufferings he endured restored hope
to a fallen world.
Let sin never ensnare us
with empty promises of passing joy.
Make us one with you always,
so that our joy may be holy,
and our love may give life.

FIRST READING   A reading from the prophet Zechariah

See now, your king comes humbly to you.   *Zechariah 9:9-10*

The Lord says this: "Rejoice heart and soul, daughter of Zion! Shout with gladness, daughter of Jerusalem! See now, your king comes to you; he is victorious, he is triumphant, humble and riding on a donkey, on a colt, the foal of a donkey. He will banish chariots from Ephraim and horses from Jerusalem; the bow of war will be banished. He will proclaim peace for the nations. His empire shall stretch from sea to sea, from the river to the ends of the earth."
This is the word of the Lord. **Thanks be to God.**

RESPONSORIAL PSALM   *Psalm 144*
I will bless your name for ever,
O God my King.
or **Alleluia!**

1. I will give you glory, O God
     my King,
   I will bless your name for ever.
   I will bless you day after day
   and praise your name for ever.

2. The Lord is kind and full
     of compassion,
   slow to anger, abounding in love.
   How good is the Lord to all,
   compassionate to all his creatures.

3. All your creatures shall thank you,
   O Lord,
   and your friends shall repeat
     their blessing.
   They shall speak of the glory of your reign
   and declare your might, O God.

4. The Lord is faithful in all his words
   and loving in all his deeds.
   The Lord supports all who fall
   and raises all who are bowed down.

SECOND READING   A reading from the letter of St Paul to the Romans

If by the Spirit you put an end to the misdeeds of the body you will live.

Romans 8:9,11-13

Your interests are not in the unspiritual, but in the spiritual, since the Spirit of God has made his home in you. In fact, unless you possessed the Spirit of Christ you would not belong to him, and if the Spirit of him who raised Jesus from the dead is living in you, then he who raised Jesus from the dead will give life to your own mortal bodies through his Spirit living in you.

So then, my brothers, there is no necessity for us to obey our unspiritual selves or to live unspiritual lives. If you do live in that way, you are doomed to die; but if by the Spirit you put an end to the misdeeds of the body you will live.

This is the word of the Lord. **Thanks be to God.**

All stand to greet the Gospel. If this Acclamation is not sung it may be omitted.

Alleluia, alleluia! Blessed are you, Father, Lord of heaven and earth, for revealing the mysteries of the kingdom to mere children. Alleluia!

GOSPEL   *Matthew 11:25-30*

The Lord be with you. **And also with you.**

A reading from the holy Gospel according to Matthew. **Glory to you, Lord.**

I am gentle and humble in heart.

Jesus exclaimed, "I bless you, Father, Lord of heaven and of earth, for hiding these things from the learned and the clever and revealing them to mere children. Yes, Father, for that is what it pleased you to do. Everything has been entrusted to me by my Father; and no one knows the Son except the Father, just as no one knows the Father except the Son and those to whom the Son chooses to reveal him.

"Come to me, all you who labour and are overburdened, and I will give you rest. Shoulder my yoke and learn from me, for I am gentle and humble in heart, and you will find rest for your souls. Yes, my yoke is easy and my burden light."

This is the Gospel of the Lord. **Praise to you, Lord Jesus Christ.**

The Homily follows, then | *Turn to page 6 for the Creed* |

PRAYER OVER THE GIFTS

Lord,
let this offering to the glory of your name
purify us and bring us closer
   to eternal life.

Turn to pages 8-10 for the Preface and Eucharistic Prayer

COMMUNION ANTIPHON
Taste and see the goodness of the Lord;
blessed is he who hopes in God.

Come to me, all you that labour and are
burdened, and I will give you rest, says
the Lord.

PRAYER AFTER COMMUNION
Lord,
may we never fail to praise you
for the fullness of life and salvation
you give us in this eucharist.

Turn to page 21 for the Concluding Rite

15th Sunday in Ordinary Time

As the priest goes to the altar everyone joins in this Entrance Antiphon or a hymn.

In my justice I shall see your face, O Lord; when your glory appears, my joy will be full.

Turn to page 4

OPENING PRAYER
God our Father,
your light of truth
guides us to the way of Christ.
May all who follow him
reject what is contrary to the Gospel.

Father,
let the light of your truth
guide us to your kingdom
through a world filled with lights
contrary to your own.
Christian is the name and the gospel we
glory in.
May your love make us what you have
called us to be.

FIRST READING   A reading from the prophet Isaiah

The rain makes the earth give growth.   *Isaiah 55:10-11*

Thus says the Lord: "As the rain and the snow come down from the heavens and do not return without watering the earth, making it yield and giving growth to provide seed for the sower and bread for the eating, so the word that goes from my mouth does not return to me empty, without carrying out my will and succeeding in what it was sent to do." This is the word of the Lord. **Thanks be to God.**

RESPONSORIAL PSALM   *Psalm 64*
Some seed fell into rich soil,
and produced its crop.

1. You care for the earth, give it water,
   you fill it with riches.
   Your river in heaven brims over
   to provide its grain.

2. And thus you provide for the earth;
   you drench its furrows,
   you level it, soften it with showers,
   you bless its growth.

3. You crown the year with your goodness.
Abundance flows in your steps,
in the pastures of the wilderness it flows.

4. The hills are girded with joy,
the meadows covered with flocks
the valleys are decked with wheat.
They shout for joy, yes, they sing.

SECOND READING   A reading from the letter of St Paul to the Romans
The whole creation is eagerly waiting for God to reveal his sons.   *Roman 8:18-23*

I think that what we suffer in this life can never be compared to the glory, as yet unrevealed, which is waiting for us. The whole creation is eagerly waiting for God to reveal his sons. It was not for any fault on the part of creation that it was made unable to attain its purpose, it has made so by God; but creation still retains the hope of being freed, like us, from its slavery to decadence, to enjoy the same freedom and glory as the children of God. From the beginning till now the entire creation, as we know, has been groaning in one great act of giving birth; and not only creation, but all of us who possess the first-fruits of the Spirit, we too groan inwardly as we wait for our bodies to be set free.
This is the word of the Lord. **Thanks be to God.**

All stand to greet the Gospel. If this Acclamation is not sung it may be omitted.
Alleluia, alleluia! Speak, Lord, your servant is listening; you have the message of eternal life. Alleluia!

or **Alleluia, alleluia! The seed is the word of God, Christ the sower; whoever finds this seed will remain for ever. Alleluia!**

GOSPEL   *Matthew 13:1-23 (or: 13:1-9)*
The Lord be with you. **And also with you.**
A reading from the holy Gospel according to Matthew. **Glory to you, Lord.**

A sower went out to sow.

Jesus left the house and sat by the lakeside, but such crowds gathered round him that he got into a boat and sat there. The people all stood on the beach, and he told them many things in parables. He said, "Imagine a sower going out to sow. As he sowed some seeds fell on the edge of the path, and the birds came and ate them up. Others fell on patches of rock where they found little soil and sprang up straight away, because there was no depth of earth; but as soon as the sun came up they were scorched and, not having any roots, they withered away. Others fell among thorns, and the thorns grew up and choked them. Others fell on rich soil and produced their crop, some a hundredfold, some sixty, some thirty. Listen, anyone who has ears!"
Then the disciples went up to him and asked, "Why do you talk to them in parables?" "Because," he replied, "the mysteries of the kingdom of heaven are revealed to you, but they are not revealed to them. For anyone who has will be given more, and he will have more than enough; but from anyone who has not, even what he has will be taken away. The reason I talk to them in parables is that they look without seeing and listen without hearing or understanding. So in their case this prophecy of Isaiah is being fulfilled: You will listen and listen again, but not understand, see and see again, but not perceive. For the heart of this nation has grown coarse, their ears are dull of hearing, and they have shut their eyes, for fear they should see with their eyes, hear with their ears, understand with their heart, and be converted and be healed by me. But happy are your eyes because they see, your ears because they hear! I tell you solemnly,

many prophets and holy men longed to see what you see, and never saw it; to hear what you hear, and never heard it. You, therefore, are to hear the parable of the sower. When anyone hears the word of the kingdom without understanding, the evil one comes and carries off what was sown in his heart: this is the man who received the seed on the edge of the path. The one who received it on patches of rock is the man who hears the word and welcomes it at once with joy. But he has no root in him, he does not last; let some trial come, or some persecution on account of the word, and he falls away at once. The one who received the seed in thorns is the man who hears the word, but the worries of this world and the lure of riches choke the word and so he produces nothing. And the one who received the seed in rich soil is the man who hears the word and understands it; he is the one who yields a harvest and produces now a hundredfold, now sixty, now thirty."
This is the Gospel of the Lord. **Praise to you, Lord Jesus Christ.**

The Homily follows, then   *Turn to page 6 for the Creed*

PRAYER OVER THE GIFTS
Lord,
accept the gifts of your Church.
May this eucharist
help us grow in holiness and faith.

Turn to pages 8-10 for the Preface and Eucharistic Prayer

COMMUNION ANTIPHON
The sparrow even finds a home, the swallow finds a nest wherein to place her young, near to your altars, Lord of hosts, my King, my God! How happy they who dwell in your house! For ever they are praising you.

Whoever eats my flesh and drinks my blood will live in me and I in him, says the Lord.

PRAYER AFTER COMMUNION
Lord,
by our sharing in the mystery of
    this eucharist,
let your saving love grow within us.

Turn to page 21 for the Concluding Rite

16th Sunday in Ordinary Time

As the priest goes to the altar everyone joins in this Entrance Antiphon or a hymn.

God himself is my help. The Lord up-holds my life. I will offer you a willing sacrifice; I will praise your name, O Lord, for its goodness.

Turn to page 4

OPENING PRAYER
Lord,
be merciful to your people.
Fill us with your gifts
and make us always eager to serve you
in faith, hope, and love.

Father,
let the gift of your life
continue to grow in us,
drawing us from death to faith, hope,
and love.
Keep us alive in Christ Jesus.
Keep us watchful in prayer
and true to his teaching
till your glory is revealed in us.

FIRST READING   A reading from the book of Wisdom
After sin you will grant repentance.   *Wisdom 12:13,16-19*

There is no god, other than you, who cares for everything, to whom you might have to prove that you never judged unjustly. Your justice has its source in strength, your sovereignty over all makes you lenient to all. You show your strength when your sovereign power is questioned and you expose the insolence of those who know it; but, disposing of such strength, you are mild in judgement, you govern us with great lenience, for you have only to will, and your power is there. By acting thus you have taught a lesson to your people how the virtuous man must be kindly to his fellow men, and you have given your sons the good hope that after sin you will grant repentance. This is the word of the Lord. **Thanks be to God.**

RESPONSORIAL PSALM   *Psalm 85*
O Lord, you are good and forgiving.

1. O Lord, you are good and forgiving,
   full of love to all who call.
   Give heed, O Lord, to my prayer
   and attend to the sound of my voice.

2. All the nations shall come to adore you
   and glorify your name, O Lord:
   for you are great and do marvellous deeds,
   you who alone are God.

3. But you, God of mercy and compassion,
   slow to anger, O Lord,
   abounding in love and truth,
   turn and take pity on me.

SECOND READING   A reading from the letter of St Paul to the Romans
The Spirit expresses our plea in a way that could never be put into words.
                                                          Romans 8:26-27

The Spirit comes to help us in our weakness. For when we cannot choose words in order to pray properly, the Spirit himself expresses our plea in a way that could never be put into words, and God who knows everything in our hearts knows perfectly well what he means, and that the pleas of the saints expressed by the Spirit are according to the mind of God.
This is the word of the Lord. **Thanks be to God.**

All stand to greet the Gospel. If this Acclamation is not sung it may be omitted.
Alleluia, alleluia! May the Father of our Lord Jesus Christ enlighten the eyes of our mind, so that we can see what hope his call holds for us. Alleluia!
or **Alleluia, alleluia! Blessed are you, Father, Lord of heaven and earth, for revealing the mysteries of the kingdom to mere children. Alleluia!**

GOSPEL   *Matthew 13:24-43 (or: 13:24-30)*
The Lord be with you. **And also with you.**
A reading from the holy Gospel according to Matthew. **Glory to you, Lord.**
Let them grow together until the harvest.

Jesus put a parable before the crowds, "The kingdom of heaven may be compared to a man who sowed good seed in his field. While everybody was asleep his enemy came, sowed darnel all among the wheat, and made off. When the new wheat sprouted and ripened, the darnel appeared as well. The owner's servant went to him and said, 'Sir, was it not good seed that you sowed in your field? If so, where does the darnel come from?' 'Some enemy has done this,' he answered. And the servant said 'Do you want us to go and weed it out?' But he said, 'No, because when you weed out the darnel you might pull up the wheat with it. Let them both grow till the harvest; and at harvest time I shall say to the reapers: first collect the darnel and tie it in bundles to be burnt, then gather the wheat into my barn.' "
He put another parable before them, "The kingdom of heaven is like a mustard seed which a man took and sowed in his field. It is the smallest of all the seeds, but when it has grown it is the biggest shrub of all and becomes a tree so that the birds of the air come and shelter in its branches."
He told them another parable, "The kingdom of heaven is like the yeast a woman took and mixed in with three measures of flour till it was leavened all through."
In all this Jesus spoke to the crowds in parables; indeed, he would never speak to them except in parables. This was to fulfil the prophecy: I will speak to you in parables and expound things hidden since the foundation of the world.
Then, leaving the crowds, he went to the house; and his disciples came to him and said, "Explain the parable about the darnel in the field to us." He said in reply, "The sower of the good seed is the Son of Man. The field is the world; the good seed is the subjects of the kingdom; the darnel, the subjects of the evil one; the enemy who sowed them, the devil; the harvest is the end of the world; the reapers are the angels. Well then, just as the darnel is gathered up and burnt in the fire, so it will be at the end of time. The Son of Man will send his angels and they will gather out of his kingdom all things that provoke offences and all who do evil, and throw them into the blazing furnace, where there will be weeping and grinding of teeth. Then the virtuous will shine like the sun in the kingdom of their Father. Listen, anyone who has ears!"
This is the Gospel of the Lord. **Praise to you, Lord Jesus Christ**

The Homily follows, then   Turn to page 6 for the Creed

PRAYER OVER THE GIFTS
Lord,
bring us closer to salvation
through these gifts which we bring
    in your honour.
Accept the perfect sacrifice you have
    given us,
bless it as you blessed the gifts of Abel.

Turn to pages 8-10 for the Preface and Eucharistic Prayer

COMMUNION ANTIPHON

The Lord keeps in our minds the wonderful things he has done. He is compassion and love; he always provides for his faithful.

I stand at the door and knock, says the Lord. If anyone hears my voice and opens the door, I will come in and sit down to supper with him, and he with me.

PRAYER AFTER COMMUNION
Merciful Father,
may these mysteries
give us new purpose
and bring us to a new life in you.

Turn to page 21 for the Concluding Rite

17th Sunday in Ordinary Time

As the priest goes to the altar everyone joins in this Entrance Antiphon or a hymn.
God is in his holy dwelling; he will give a home to the lonely, he gives power and strength to his people.

Turn to page 4

OPENING PRAYER

God our Father and protector,
without you nothing is holy,
nothing has value.
Guide us to everlasting life
by helping us to use wisely
the blessings you have given
    to the world.

God our Father,
open our eyes to see your hand at work
in the splendour of creation,
in the beauty of human life.
Touched by your hand our world is holy.
Help us to cherish the gifts that surround us,
to share your blessings with our brothers and sisters,
and to experience the joy of life in your presence.

FIRST READING   A reading from the first book of Kings

You have asked for a discerning judgement for yourself.   *1 Kings 3:5,7-12*

The Lord appeared in a dream to Solomon. God said, "Ask what you would like me to give you." Solomon replied, "Lord, my God, you have made your servant king in succession to David my father. But I am a very young man, unskilled in leadership. Your servant finds himself in the midst of this people of yours that you have chosen, a people so many its numbers cannot be counted or reckoned. Give your servant a heart to understand how to discern between good and evil, for who could govern this people of yours that is so great?" It pleased the Lord that Solomon should have asked for this. "Since you have asked for this," the Lord said, "and not for long life for yourself or riches or the lives of your enemies, but have asked for a discerning judgement for yourself, here and now I do what you ask. I give you a heart wise and shrewd as none before you has had and none will have after you."
This is the word of the Lord. **Thanks be to God.**

RESPONSORIAL PSALM *Psalm 118*
Lord, how I love your law!

1. My part, I have resolved, O Lord,
   is to obey your word.
   The law from your mouth means
      more to me
   than silver and gold.

2. Let your love be ready to console me
   by your promise to your servant.
   Let your love come to me and I shall live,
   for your law is my delight.

3. That is why I love your commands
   more than finest gold.
   That is why I rule my life by
      your precepts:
   I hate false ways.

4. Your will is wonderful indeed;
   therefore I obey it.
   The unfolding of your word gives light
   and teaches the simple.

SECOND READING A reading from the letter of St Paul to the Romans

God intended us to become true images of his Son. *Romans 8:28-30*

We know that by turning everything to their good God co-operates with all those who love him, with all those that he has called according to his purpose. They are the ones he chose specially long ago and intended to become true images of his Son, so that his Son might be the eldest of many brothers. He called those he intended for this; those he called he justified, and with those he justified he shared his glory.
This is the word of the Lord. **Thanks be to God.**

All stand to greet the Gospel. If this Acclamation is not sung it may be omitted.
Alleluia, alleluia! I call you friends says the Lord, because I have made known to you everything I have learnt from my Father. Alleluia!

or **Alleluia, alleluia! Blessed are you, Father, Lord of heaven and earth, for revealing the mysteries of the kingdom to mere children.**

GOSPEL *Matthew 13:44-52 (or: 13:44-46)*
The Lord be with you. **And also with you.**
A reading from the holy Gospel according to Matthew. **Glory to you, Lord.**

He sells everything he owns and buys the field.

Jesus said to the crowds, "The kingdom of heaven is like treasure hidden in a field which someone has found; he hides it again, goes off happy, sells everything he owns and buys the field. Again, the kingdom of heaven is like a merchant looking for fine pearls; when he finds one of great value he goes and sells everything he owns and buys it. Again, the kingdom of heaven is like a dragnet cast into the sea that brings in a haul of all kinds. When it is full, the fishermen haul it ashore; then, sitting down, they collect the good ones in a basket and throw away those that are no use. This is how it will be at the end of time: the angels will appear and separate the wicked from the just to throw them into the blazing furnace where there will be weeping and grinding of teeth. Have you understood all this?" They said, "Yes." And he said to them, "Well, then, every scribe who becomes a disciple of the kingdom of heaven is like a householder who brings out from his storeroom things both new and old."
This is the Gospel of the Lord. **Praise to you, Lord Jesus Christ.**

The Homily follows, then Turn to page 6 for the Creed

PRAYER OVER THE GIFTS
Lord,
receive these offerings
chosen from your many gifts.
May these mysteries make us holy
and lead us to eternal joy.

Turn to pages 8-10 for the Preface and Eucharistic Prayer

COMMUNION ANTIPHON
Oh, bless the Lord, my soul, and remember all his kindness.

Happy are those who show mercy; mercy shall be theirs. Happy are the pure of heart, for they shall see God.

PRAYER AFTER COMMUNION
Lord,
we receive the sacrament
which celebrates the memory
of the death and resurrection of Christ
    your Son.
May this gift bring us closer to our
    eternal salvation.

Turn to page 21 for the Concluding Rite

18th Sunday in Ordinary Time

As the priest goes to the altar everyone joins in this Entrance Antiphon or a hymn.

God, come to my help. Lord, quickly give me assistance. You are the one who helps me and sets me free: Lord, do not be long in coming.

Turn to page 4

OPENING PRAYER
Father of everlasting goodness,
our origin and guide,
be close to us
and hear the prayer of all who praise you.
Forgive our sins and restore us to life.
Keep us safe in your love.

God our Father,
gifts without measure flow from your goodness
to bring us peace.
Our life is your gift.
Guide our life's journey,
for only your love makes us whole.
Keep us strong in your love.

FIRST READING   A reading from the book of the prophet Isaiah
Come and eat.   *Isaiah 55:1-3*

Thus says the Lord: Oh, come to the water all you who are thirsty; though you have no money, come! Buy corn without money, and eat, and, at no cost, wine and milk. Why spend money on what is not bread, your wages on what fails to satisfy? Listen, listen to me and you will have good things to eat and rich food to enjoy. Pay attention, come to me; listen, and your soul will live. With you I will make an everlasting covenant out of the favours promised to David.
This is the word of the Lord. **Thanks be to God.**

RESPONSORIAL PSALM   *Psalm 144*
You open wide your hand, O Lord, you grant our desires.

1. The Lord is kind and full
    of compassion,
    slow to anger, abounding in love,
    how good is the Lord to all,
    compassionate to all his creatures.

2. The eyes of all creatures look to you
    and you give them their food in due time.
    You open wide your hand,
    grant the desires of all who live.

3. The Lord is just in all his ways
    and loving in all his deeds.
    He is close to all who call him,
    who call on him from their hearts.

SECOND READING   A reading from the letter of St Paul to the Romans
No created thing can ever come between us and the love of God made visible in Christ.
                                                            Romans 8:35,37-39

Nothing can come between us and the love of Christ, even if we are troubled or worried, or being persecuted, or lacking food or clothes, or being threatened or even attacked. These are the trials through which we triumph, by the power of him who loved us. For I am certain of this: neither death nor life, no angel, no prince, nothing that exists, nothing still to come, not any power, or height or depth, nor any created thing, can ever come between us and the love of God made visible in Christ our Lord.
This is the word of the Lord. **Thanks be to God.**

All stand to greet the Gospel. If this Acclamation is not sung it may be omitted.
Alleluia, alleluia! Blessings on the King who comes, in the name of the Lord! Peace in heaven and glory in the highest heavens! Alleluia!

or **Alleluia, alleluia! Man does not live on bread alone, but on every word that comes from the mouth of God.**

GOSPEL   *Matthew 14:13-21*
The Lord be with you. **And also with you.**
A reading from the holy Gospel according to Matthew. **Glory to you, Lord.**
They all ate as much as they wanted.

When Jesus received the news of John the Baptist's death he withdrew by boat to a lonely place where they could be by themselves. But the people heard of this and, leaving the towns, went after him on foot. So as he stepped ashore he saw a large crowd; and he took pity on them and healed their sick.
When evening came, the disciples went to him and said, "This is a lonely place, and the time has slipped by; so send the people away, and they can go to the villages to buy themselves some food." Jesus replied, "There is no need for them to go: give them something to eat yourselves." But they answered, "All we have with us is five loaves and two fish." "Bring them here to me," he said. He gave orders that the people were to sit down on the grass; then he took the five loaves and the two fish, raised his eyes to heaven and said the blessing. And breaking the loaves he handed them to his disciples who gave them to the crowds. They all ate as much as they wanted, and they collected the scraps remaining, twelve baskets full. Those who ate numbered about five thousand men, to say nothing of women and children.
This is the Gospel of the Lord. **Praise to you, Lord Jesus Christ.**

The Homily follows, then | Turn to page 6 for the Creed |

PRAYER OVER THE GIFTS
Merciful Lord,
make holy these gifts,
and let our spiritual sacrifice
make us an everlasting gift to you.

Turn to pages 8-10 for the Preface and Eucharistic Prayer

COMMUNION ANTIPHON
You gave us bread from heaven, Lord: a sweet-tasting bread that was very good to eat.

The Lord says: I am the bread of life. A man who comes to me will not go away hungry, and no one who believes in me will thirst.

PRAYER AFTER COMMUNION
Lord, you give us the strength of new life
by the gift of the eucharist.
Protect us with your love
and prepare us for eternal redemption.

Turn to page 21 for the Concluding Rite

19th Sunday in Ordinary Time

As the priest goes to the altar everyone joins in this Entrance Antiphon or a hymn.

Lord, be true to your covenant, forget not the life of your poor ones for ever. Rise up, O God, and defend your cause; do not ignore the shouts of your enemies.

Turn to page 4

OPENING PRAYER
Almighty and ever-living God
your Spirit made us your children,
confident to call you Father.
Increase your Spirit within us
and bring us to our promised inheritance.

Father,
we come, reborn in the spirit,
to celebrate our sonship in the Lord Jesus
Christ.
Touch our hearts,
help them grow toward the life you have
promised.
Touch our lives,
make them signs of your love for all men.

FIRST READING   A reading from the first book of Kings

Stand on the mountain before the Lord.   *1 Kings 19:9,11-13*

When Elijah reached Horeb, the mountain of God, he went into the cave and spent the night in it. Then he was told, "Go out and stand on the mountain before the Lord." Then the Lord himself went by. There came a mighty wind, so strong it tore the

mountains and shattered the rocks before the Lord. But the Lord was not in the wind. After the wind came an earthquake. But the Lord was not in the earthquake. After the earthquake came a fire. But the Lord was not in the fire. And after the fire came the sound of a gentle breeze. And when Elijah heard this, he covered his face with his cloak and went out and stood at the entrance of the cave.
This is the word of the Lord. **Thanks be to God.**

RESPONSORIAL PSALM *Psalm 84*
Let us see, O Lord, your mercy

and give us your saving help.

1. I will hear what the Lord God has to say, a voice that speaks of peace.
His help is near for those who fear him and his glory will dwell in our land.

2. Mercy and faithfulness have met; justice and peace have embraced.
Faithfulness shall spring from the earth and justice look down from heaven.

3. The Lord will make us prosper and our earth shall yield its fruit.
Justice shall march before him and peace shall follow his steps.

SECOND READING A reading from the letter of St Paul to the Romans

I would willingly be condemned if it could help my brothers. *Romans 9:1-5*

What I want to say is no pretence; I say it in union with Christ – it is the truth – my conscience in union with the Holy Spirit assures me of it too. What I want to say is this: my sorrow is so great, my mental anguish so endless, I would willingly be condemned and be cut off from Christ if it could help my brothers of Israel, my own flesh and blood. They were adopted as sons, they were given the glory and the covenants; the Law and the ritual were drawn up for them, and the promises were made to them. They are descended from the patriarchs and from their flesh and blood came Christ who is above all, God for ever blessed! Amen.
This is the word of the Lord. **Thanks be to God.**

All stand to greet the Gospel. If this Acclamation is not sung it may be omitted.
Alleluia, alleluia! Blessings on the King who comes, in the name of the Lord! Peace in heaven and glory in the highest heavens! Alleluia!
or **Alleluia, alleluia! My soul is waiting for the Lord, I count on his word. Alleluia!**

GOSPEL *Matthew 14:22-23*
The Lord be with you. **And also with you.**
A reading from the holy Gospel according to Matthew. **Glory to you, Lord.**

Tell me to come to you across the water.

Jesus made the disciples get into the boat and go on ahead to the other side while he would send the crowds away. After sending the crowds away he went up into the hills by himself to pray. When evening came, he was there alone, while the boat, by now far out on the lake, was battling with a heavy sea, for there was a headwind. In the fourth watch of the night he went towards them, walking on the lake, and when the disciples saw him walking on the lake they were terrified. "It is a ghost," they said, and cried out in fear. But at once Jesus called to them, saying, "Courage! It is I! Do not be afraid." It was Peter who answered. "Lord," he said, "if it is you, tell me to

come to you across the water." "Come," said Jesus. Then Peter got out of the boat and started walking towards Jesus across the water, but as soon as he felt the force of the wind, he took fright and began to sink. "Lord! Save me!" he cried. Jesus put out his hand at once and held him. "Man of little faith," he said, "why did you doubt?" And as they got into the boat the wind dropped. The men in the boat bowed down before him and said, "Truly, you are the Son of God."
This is the Gospel of the Lord. **Praise to you, Lord Jesus Christ.**

The Homily follows, then   Turn to page 6 for the Creed

PRAYER OVER THE GIFTS
God of power,
giver of the gifts we bring,
accept the offering of your Church
and make it the sacrament of our salvation.

Turn to pages 8-10 for the Preface and Eucharistic Prayer

COMMUNION ANTIPHON
Praise the Lord, Jerusalem; he feeds you with the finest wheat.

The bread I shall give is my flesh for the life of the world, says the Lord.

PRAYER AFTER COMMUNION
Lord,
may the eucharist you give us
bring us to salvation
and keep us faithful to the light
    of your truth.

Turn to page 21 for the Concluding Rite

20th Sunday in Ordinary Time

As the priest goes to the altar everyone joins in this Entrance Antiphon or a hymn.
God, our protector, keep us in mind; always give strength to your people. For if we can be with you even one day, it is better than a thousand without you.

Turn to page 4

OPENING PRAYER
God our Father,
may we love you in all things and above
    all things
and reach the joy you have prepared
    for us
beyond all our imagining.

Almighty God, ever-loving Father,
your care extends beyond the
boundaries of race and nation
to the hearts of all who live.

May the walls, which prejudice raises
between us,
crumble beneath the shadow of your
outstretched arm.

FIRST READING A reading from the book of the prophet Isaiah
I will bring foreigners to my holy mountain. *Isaiah 56:1,6-7*

Thus says the Lord: Have a care for justice, act with integrity, for soon my salvation will come and my integrity be manifest.
Foreigners who have attached themselves to the Lord to serve him and to love his name and be his servants – all who observe the sabbath, not profaning it and cling to my covenant – these I will bring to my holy mountain. I will make them joyful in my house of prayer. Their holocausts and their sacrifices will be accepted on my altar, for my house will be called a house of prayer for all the peoples.
This is the word of the Lord. **Thanks be to God.**

RESPONSORIAL PSALM *Psalm 66*
Let the peoples praise you, O God;
let all the peoples praise you.

1. O God, be gracious and bless us
and let your face shed its light upon us.
So will your ways be known upon earth
and all nations learn your saving help.

2. Let the nations be glad and exult
for you rule the world with justice.
With fairness you rule the peoples,
you guide the nations on earth.

3. Let the peoples praise you, O God;
let all the peoples praise you.
May God still give us his blessing
till the ends of the earth revere him.

SECOND READING A reading from the letter of St Paul to the Romans
With Israel, God never takes back his gifts or revokes his choice.
Romans 11:13-15,29-32

Let me tell you pagans this: I have been sent to the pagans as their apostle, and I am proud of being sent, but the purpose of it is to make my own people envious of you, and in this way save some of them. Since their rejection meant the reconciliation of the world, do you know what their admission will mean? Nothing less than a resurrection from the dead! God never takes back his gifts or revokes his choice. Just as you changed from being disobedient to God, and now enjoy mercy because of their disobedience, so those who are disobedient now – and only because of the mercy shown to you – will also enjoy mercy eventually. God has imprisoned all men in their own disobedience only to show mercy to all mankind.
This is the word of the Lord. **Thanks be to God.**

All stand to greet the Gospel. If this Acclamation is not sung it may be omitted.
Alleluia, alleluia! The sheep that belong to me listen to my voice, says the Lord, I know them and they follow me. Alleluia!

or **Alleluia, alleluia! Jesus proclaimed the Good News of the kingdom, and cured all kinds of sickness among the people. Alleluia!**

GOSPEL *Matthew 15:21-28*
The Lord be with you. **And also with you.**
A reading from the holy Gospel according to Matthew. **Glory to you, Lord.**
Woman you have great faith.

Jesus left Gennesaret and withdrew to the region of Tyre and Sidon. Then out came a Canaanite woman from that district and started shouting, "Sir, Son of David, take pity on me. My daughter is tormented by a devil." But he answered her not a word. And his disciples went and pleaded with him. "Give her what she wants," they said, "because she is shouting after us." He said in reply, "I was sent only to the lost sheep of the House of Israel." But the woman had come up and was kneeling at his feet. "Lord," she said, "help me." He replied, "It is not fair to take the children's food and throw it to the house-dogs." She retorted, "Ah yes, sir; but even house-dogs can eat the scraps that fall from their master's table." Then Jesus answered her, "Woman you have great faith. Let your wish be granted." And from that moment her daughter was well again. This is the Gospel of the Lord. **Praise to you, Lord Jesus Christ.**

The Homily follows, then Turn to page 6 for the Creed

PRAYER OVER THE GIFTS
Lord,
accept our sacrifice
as a holy exchange of gifts.
By offering what you have given us
may we receive the gift of yourself.

Turn to pages 8-10 for the Preface and Eucharistic Prayer

COMMUNION ANTIPHON
With the Lord there is mercy, and fullness of redemption.

I am the living bread from heaven, says the Lord; if anyone eats this bread he will live for ever.

PRAYER AFTER COMMUNION
God of mercy,
by this sacrament you make us one with Christ.
By becoming more like him on earth,
may we come to share his glory in heaven,
where he lives and reigns for ever and ever.

Turn to page 21 for the Concluding Rite

21st Sunday in Ordinary Time

As the priest goes to the altar everyone joins in this Entrance Antiphon or a hymn.

Listen, Lord, and answer me. Save your servant who trusts in you. I call to you all day long, have mercy on me, O Lord.

Turn to page 4

OPENING PRAYER
Father,
help us to seek the values
that will bring us lasting joy in this
    changing world.
In our desire for what you promise
make us one in mind and heart.

Lord our God,
all truth is from you,
and you alone bring oneness of heart.
Give your people the joy
of hearing your word in every sound
and of longing for your presence more than
for life itself.
May all the attractions of a changing world
serve only to bring us
the peace of your kingdom which this world
does not give.

FIRST READING   A reading from the book of the prophet Isaiah
I place the key of the House of David on his shoulder.   *Isaiah 22:19-23*

Thus says the Lord of hosts to Shebna, the master of the palace: I dismiss you from your office, I remove you from your post, and the same day I call on my servant Eliakim son of Hilkiah. I invest him with your robe, gird him with your sash, entrust him with your authority; and he shall be a father to the inhabitants of Jerusalem and to the House of Judah. I place the key of the House of David on his shoulder; should he open, no one shall close, should he close, no one shall open. I drive him like a peg into a firm place; he will become a throne of glory for his father's house.
This is the word of the Lord. **Thanks be to God.**

RESPONSORIAL PSALM   *Psalm 137*
Your love, O Lord, is eternal, discard not the work of your hands.

1. I thank you, Lord, with all my heart,
   you have heard the words of my mouth.
   Before the angels I will bless you.
   I will adore before your holy temple.

2. I thank you for your faithfulness
   and love
   which excel all we ever knew of you.
   On the day I called, you answered;
   you increased the strength of my soul.

3. The Lord is high yet he looks on the lowly
   and the haughty he knows from afar.
   Your love, O Lord, is eternal
   discard not the work of your hands.

SECOND READING   A reading from the letter of St Paul to the Romans
All that exists comes from him; all is by him and for him.   *Romans 11:33-36*

How rich are the depths of God – how deep his wisdom and knowledge – and how impossible to penetrate his motives or understand his methods! Who could ever know the mind of the Lord? Who could ever be his counsellor? Who could ever give him anything or lend him anything? All that exists comes from him; all is by him and for him. To him be glory for ever! Amen.
This is the word of the Lord. **Thanks be to God.**

*All stand to greet the Gospel. If this Acclamation is not sung it may be omitted.**
Alleluia, alleluia! God in Christ was reconciling the world to himself, and he has entrusted to us the news that they are reconciled. Alleluia!
or **Alleluia, alleluia! You are Peter and on this rock I will build my Church. And the gates of the underworld can never hold out against it. Alleluia!**

**Previous editions of this book had the following acclamation:* Your words are spirit, Lord, and they are life: you have the message of eternal life.

GOSPEL   *Matthew 16:13-20*
The Lord be with you. **And also with you.**
A reading from the holy Gospel according to Matthew. **Glory to you, Lord.**

You are Peter, and I will give you the keys of the kingdom of heaven.

When Jesus came to the region of Caesarea Philippi he put this question to his disciples, "Who do people say the Son of Man is?" And they said, "Some say he is John the Baptist, some Elijah, and others Jeremiah or one of the prophets." "But you," he said,

"who do you say I am?" Then Simon Peter spoke up, "You are the Christ", he said, "the Son of the living God." Jesus replied, "Simon son of Jonah, you are a happy man! Because it was not flesh and blood that revealed this to you but my Father in heaven. So I now say to you: You are Peter and on this rock I will build my Church. And the gates of the underworld can never hold out against it. I will give you the keys of the kingdom of heaven: whatever you bind on earth shall be considered bound in heaven; whatever you loose on earth shall be considered loosed in heaven." Then he gave the disciples strict orders not to tell anyone that he was the Christ.
This is the Gospel of the Lord. **Praise to you, Lord Jesus Christ.**

The Homily follows, then | *Turn to page 6 for the Creed*

PRAYER OVER THE GIFTS
Merciful God,
perfect sacrifice of Jesus Christ
made us your people.
In your love,
grant peace and unity to your Church.

Turn to pages 8-10 for the Preface and Eucharistic Prayer

COMMUNION ANTIPHON
Lord, the earth is filled with your gift from heaven; man grows bread from earth, and wine to cheer his heart.

The Lord says: The man who eats my flesh and drinks my blood will live for ever; I shall raise him to life on the last day.

PRAYER AFTER COMMUNION
Lord,
may this eucharist increase within us
the healing power of your love.
May it guide and direct our efforts
to please you in all things.

Turn to page 21 for the Concluding Rite

22nd Sunday in Ordinary Time

As the priest goes to the altar everyone joins in this Entrance Antiphon or a hymn.
I call to you all day long, have mercy on me, O Lord. You are good and forgiving, full of love for all who call to you.

Turn to page 4

OPENING PRAYER
Almighty God,
every good thing comes from you.
Fill our hearts with love for you,
increase our faith,
and by your constant care
protect the good you have given us.

Lord God of power and might,
nothing is good which is against your will,
and all is of value which comes from your hand.
Place in our hearts a desire to please you
and fill our minds with insight into love,
so that every thought may grow in wisdom
and all our efforts may be filled with your peace.

FIRST READING   A reading from the prophet Jeremiah
The word of the Lord has meant insult for me.   *Jeremiah 20:7-9*

You have seduced me, Lord, and I have let myself be seduced; you have overpowered me: you were the stronger. I am a daily laughing-stock, everybody's butt. Each time I speak the word, I have to howl and proclaim: "Violence and ruin!" The word of the Lord has meant for me insult, derision, all day long. I used to say, "I will not think about him, I will not speak in his name any more." Then there seemed to be a fire burning in my heart, imprisoned in my bones. The effort to restrain it wearied me, I could not bear it.
This is the word of the Lord. **Thanks be to God.**

RESPONSORIAL PSALM   *Psalm 62*
For you my soul is thirsting, O Lord my God.

1. O God, you are my God, for you I
   long;
   for you my soul is thirsting.
   My body pines for you
   like a dry, weary land without water.

2. So I gaze on you in the sanctuary
   to see your strength and your glory.
   For your love is better than life,
   my lips will speak your praise.

3. So I will bless you all my life,
   in your name I will lift up my hands.
   My soul shall be filled as with a
   banquet,
   my mouth shall praise you with joy.

4. For you have been my help;
   in the shadow of your wings I
   rejoice.
   My soul clings to you;
   your right hand holds me fast.

SECOND READING   A reading from the letter of St Paul to the Romans
Offer your bodies as a living sacrifice.   *Romans 12:1-2*

Think of God's mercy, my brothers, and worship him, I beg you, in a way that is worthy of thinking beings, by offering your living bodies as a holy sacrifice, truly pleasing to God. Do not model yourselves on the behaviour of the world around you, but let your behaviour change, modelled by your new mind. This is the only way to discover the will of God and know what is good, what it is that God wants, what is the perfect thing to do.
This is the word of the Lord. **Thanks be to God.**

All stand to greet the Gospel. If this Acclamation is not sung it may be omitted.
Alleluia, alleluia! May the Father of our Lord Jesus Christ enlighten the eyes of our mind, so that we can see what hope his call holds for us. Alleluia!

GOSPEL   *Matthew 16:21-27*
The Lord be with you. **And also with you.**
A reading from the holy Gospel according to Matthew. **Glory to you, Lord.**

If anyone wants to be a follower of mine, let him renounce himself.

Jesus began to make it clear to his disciples that he was destined to go to Jerusalem and suffer grievously at the hands of the elders and chief priests and scribes, to be put to death and to be raised up on the third day. Then, taking him aside, Peter started to remonstrate with him. "Heaven preserve you, Lord," he said. "This must not happen to you." But he turned and said to Peter, "Get behind me, Satan! You are an obstacle in my path, because the way you think is not God's way but man's."

Then Jesus said to his disciples, "If anyone wants to be a follower of mine, let him renounce himself and take up his cross and follow me. For anyone who wants to save his life will lose it; but anyone who loses his life for my sake will find it. What, then, will a man gain if he wins the whole world and ruins his life? Or what has a man to offer in exchange for his life?

"For the Son of Man is going to come in the glory of his Father with his angels, and, when he does, he will reward each one according to his behaviour."

This is the Gospel of the Lord. **Praise to you, Lord Jesus Christ.**

The Homily follows then | *Turn to page 6 for the Creed* |

PRAYER OVER THE GIFTS
Lord,
may this holy offering
bring us your holy blessing
and accomplish within us
its promise of salvation.

| *Turn to pages 8-10 for the Preface and Eucharistic Prayer* |

COMMUNION ANTIPHON
O Lord, how great is the depth of the kindness which you have shown to those who love you.

Happy are the peacemakers; they shall be called the sons of God. Happy are they who suffer persecution for justice's sake; the kingdom of heaven is theirs.

PRAYER AFTER COMMUNION
Lord,
you renew us at your table with
    the bread of life.
May this food strengthen us in love
and help us to serve you in each other.

| *Turn to page 21 for the Concluding Rite* |

23rd Sunday in Ordinary Time

As the priest goes to the altar everyone joins in this Entrance Antiphon or a hymn.
Lord, you are just, and the judgements you make are right. Show mercy when you judge me, your servant.

> Turn to page 4

OPENING PRAYER
God our Father,
you redeem us
and make us your children in Christ.
Look upon us,
give us true freedom
and bring us to the inheritance
 you promised.

Lord our God,
in you justice and mercy meet.
With unparalled love you have saved us
from death
and drawn us into the circle of your life.

Open our eyes to the wonders this life
sets before us,
that we may serve you free from fear
and address you as God our Father.

FIRST READING   A reading from the prophet Ezekiel
If you do not speak to the wicked man, I will hold you responsible for his death.
Ezekiel 33:7-9

The word of the Lord was addressed to me as follows, "Son of Man, I have appointed you as sentry to the House of Israel. When you hear a word from my mouth, warn them in my name. If I say to a wicked man: Wicked wretch, you are to die, and you do not speak to warn the wicked man to renounce his ways, then he shall die for his sin, but I will hold you responsible for his death. If, however, you do warn a wicked man to renounce his ways and repent, and he does not repent, then he shall die for his sin, but you yourself will have saved your life."
This is the word of the Lord. **Thanks be to God.**

RESPONSORIAL PSALM   *Psalm 94*
O that today you would listen to his voice!
Harden not your hearts.

1. Come, ring out our joy to the Lord;
   hail the rock who saves us.
   Let us come before him giving thanks,
   with songs let us hail the Lord.

2. Come in; let us bow and bend low;
   let us kneel before the God who made us
   for he is our God and we
   the people who belong to his pasture,
   the flock that is led by his hand.

3. O that today you would listen to his voice!
   "Harden not your hearts as at Meribah,
   as on that day at Massah in the desert
   when your fathers put me to the test;
   when they tried me, though they saw my work."

SECOND READING   A reading from the letter of St Paul to the Romans

Love is the answer to every one of the commandments.   *Romans 13:8-10*

Avoid getting into debt, except the debt of mutual love. If you love your fellow men you have carried out your obligations. All the commandments: You shall not commit adultery, you shall not kill, you shall not steal, you shall not covet, and so on, are summed up in this single command: You must love your neighbour as yourself. Love is the one thing that cannot hurt your neighbour; that is why it is the answer to every one of the commandments.
This is the word of the Lord. **Thanks be to God.**

All stand to greet the Gospel. If this Acclamation is not sung it may be omitted.
Alleluia, alleluia! Your word is truth, O Lord, consecrate us in the truth. Alleluia!
or **Alleluia, alleluia! God in Christ was reconciling the world to himself, and he has entrusted to us the news that they are reconciled. Alleluia!**

GOSPEL   *Matthew 18:15-20*
The Lord be with you. **And also with you.**
A reading from the holy Gospel according to Matthew. **Glory to you, Lord.**

If he listens to you, you have won back your brother.

Jesus said to his disciples: "If your brother does something wrong, go and have it out with him alone, between your two selves. If he listens to you, you have won back your brother. If he does not listen, take one or two others along with you: the evidence of two or three witnesses is required to sustain any charge. But if he refuses to listen to these, report it to the community; and if he refuses to listen to the community, treat him like a pagan or a tax collector.
"I tell you solemnly, whatever you bind on earth shall be considered bound in heaven; whatever you loose on earth shall be considered loosed in heaven.
"I tell you solemnly once again, if two of you on earth agree to ask anything at all, it will be granted to you by my Father in heaven. For where two or three meet in my name, I shall be there with them."
This is the Gospel of the Lord. **Praise to you, Lord Jesus Christ.**

The Homily follows, then Turn to page 6 for the Creed

PRAYERS OVER THE GIFTS
God of peace and love,
may our offering bring you true worship
and make us one with you.

Turn to pages 8-10 for the Preface and Eucharistic Prayer

COMMUNION ANTIPHON
Like a deer that longs for running streams, my soul longs for you, my God. My soul is thirsting for the living God.

I am the light of the world, says the Lord; the man who follows me will have the light of life.

PRAYER AFTER COMMUNION
Lord,
Your word and your sacrament
give us food and life.
May this gift of your Son
lead us to share his life for ever.

Turn to page 21 for the Concluding Rite

24th Sunday in Ordinary Time

As the priest goes to the altar everyone joins in this Entrance Antiphon or a hymn.

Give peace, Lord, to those who wait for you and your prophets will proclaim you as you deserve. Hear the prayers of your servant and of your people Israel.

Turn to page 4

OPENING PRAYER
Almighty God,
our creator and guide,
may we serve you with all our heart
and know your forgiveness in our lives.

Father in heaven, creator of all,
look down upon your people in their
moments of need,
for you alone are the source of our peace.
Bring us to the dignity which
distinguishes the poor in spirit
and show us how great is the call to serve,
that we may share in the peace of Christ
who offered his life in the service of all.

FIRST READING   A reading from the book of Ecclesiasticus
Forgive your neighbour the hurt he does you, and when you pray, your sins will be forgiven.   *Ecclesiasticus 27:30-28:7*

Resentment and anger, these are foul things, and both are found with the sinner. He who exacts vengeance will experience the vengeance of the Lord, who keeps strict account of sin. Forgive your neighbour the hurt he does you, and when you pray, your sins will be forgiven. If a man nurses anger against another, can he then demand compassion from the Lord? Showing no pity for a man like himself, can he then plead for his own sins? Mere creature of flesh, he cherishes resentment; who will forgive him his sins? Remember the last things, and stop hating, remember dissolution and death, and live by the commandments. Remember the commandments, and do not bear your neighbour ill-will; remember the covenant of the Most High, and overlook the offence.
This is the word of the Lord. **Thanks be to God.**

RESPONSORIAL PSALM   *Psalm 102*

**The Lord is compassion and love,
slow to anger and rich in mercy.**

1. My soul, give thanks to the Lord,
all my being, bless his holy name.
My soul, give thanks to the Lord
and never forget all his blessings.

2. It is he who forgives all your guilt,
who heals every one of your ills,
who redeems your life from the grave,
who crowns you with love and
compassion.

3. His wrath will come to an end;
he will not be angry for ever.
He does not treat us according to our sins
nor repay us according to our faults.

4. For as the heavens are high above
the earth
so strong is his love for those who fear him
As far as the east is from the west
so far does he remove our sins.

SECOND READING   A reading from the letter of St Paul to the Romans
Alive or dead we belong to the Lord.   *Romans 14:7-9*

The life and death of each of us has its influence on others; if we live, we live for the Lord; and if we die, we die for the Lord, so that alive or dead we belong to the Lord. This explains why Christ both died and came to life, it was so that he might be Lord both of the dead and of the living.
This is the word of the Lord. **Thanks be to God.**

All stand to greet the Gospel. If this Acclamation is not sung it may be omitted
Alleluia, alleluia! Speak, Lord, your servant is listening; you have the message of eternal life. Alleluia!

or Alleluia, alleluia! I give you a new commandment: love one another, just as I have loved you, says the Lord. Alleluia!

GOSPEL   *Matthew 18:21-35*
The Lord be with you. **And also with you.**
A reading from the holy Gospel according to Matthew. **Glory to you, Lord.**

I do not tell you to forgive seven times, but seventy-seven times.

Peter went up to Jesus and said, "Lord, how often must I forgive my brother if he wrongs me? As often as seven times?" Jesus answered, "Not seven, I tell you, but seventy-seven times.
"And so the kingdom of heaven may be compared to a king who decided to settle his accounts with his servants. When the reckoning began, they brought him a man who owed ten thousand talents; but he had no means of paying, so his master gave orders that he should be sold, together with his wife and children and all his possessions, to meet the debt. At this, the servant threw himself down at his master's feet. 'Give me time,' he said, 'and I will pay the whole sum.' And the servant's master felt so sorry for him that he let him go and cancelled the debt. Now as this servant went out, he happened to meet a fellow servant who owed him one hundred denarii; and he seized him by the throat and began to throttle him. 'Pay what you owe me,' he said. His fellow servant fell at his feet and implored him, saying, 'Give me time and I will pay you.' But the other would not agree; on the contrary, he had him thrown into prison till he could pay the debt. His fellow servants were deeply distressed when they saw what had happened, and they went to their master and reported the whole affair to him. Then the master sent for him. 'You wicked servant,' he said, 'I cancelled all that debt of yours when you appealed to me. Were you not bound, then, to have pity on your fellow servant just as I had pity on you?' And in his anger the master handed him over to the torturers till he should pay all his debt. And this is how my heavenly Father will deal with you unless you each forgive your brother from your heart."
This is the Gospel of the Lord. **Praise to you, Lord Jesus Christ.**

The Homily follows, then   Turn to page 6 for the Creed

PRAYER OVER THE GIFTS
Lord,
hear the prayers of your people
and receive our gifts.
May the worship of each one here
bring salvation to all.

Turn to pages 8-10 for the Preface and Eucharistic Prayer

COMMUNION ANTIPHON

O God, how much we value your mercy! All mankind can gather under your protection.

The cup that we bless is a communion with the blood of Christ; and the bread that we break is a communion with the body of the Lord.

PRAYER AFTER COMMUNION
Lord,
may the eucharist you have given us
influence our thoughts and actions.
May your Spirit guide and direct us
in your way.

Turn to page 21 for the Concluding Rite

25th Sunday in Ordinary Time

As the priest goes to the altar everyone joins in this Entrance Antiphon or a hymn.

I am the Saviour of all people, says the Lord. Whatever their troubles, I will answer their cry, and I will always be their Lord.

Turn to page 4

OPENING PRAYER

Father,
guide us, as you guide creation
according to your law of love.
May we love one another
and come to perfection
in the eternal life prepared for us.

Father in heaven,
the perfection of justice is found in your love
and all mankind is in need of your law.
Help us to find this love in each other
that justice may be attained
through obedience to your law.

FIRST READING   A reading from the book of the prophet Isaiah

My thoughts are not your thoughts.   *Isaiah 55:6-9*

Seek the Lord while he is still to be found, call to him while he is still near. Let the wicked man abandon his way, the evil man his thoughts. Let him turn back to the Lord who will take pity on him, to our God who is rich in forgiving; for my thoughts are not your thoughts, my ways are not your ways – it is the Lord who speaks. Yes, the heavens are as high above earth as my ways are above your ways, my thoughts above your thoughts.
This is the word of the Lord. **Thanks be to God.**

RESPONSORIAL PSALM   *Psalm 144*
The Lord is close to all who call him.

1. I will bless you day after day
   and praise your name for ever.
   The Lord is great, highly to be praised,
   his greatness cannot be measured.

2. The Lord is kind and full of compassion,
   slow to anger, abounding in love.
   How good is the Lord to all,
   compassionate to all his creatures.

3. The Lord is just in all his ways
   and loving in all his deeds.
   He is close to all who call him,
   who call on him from their hearts.

SECOND READING   A reading from the letter of St Paul to the Philippians

Life to me is Christ.   *Philippians 1:20-24,27*

Christ will be glorified in my body, whether by my life or by my death. Life to me, of course, is Christ, but then death would bring me something more; but then again, if living in this body means doing work which is having good results – I do not know what I should choose. I am caught in this dilemma: I want to be gone and be with Christ, which would be very much better, but for me to stay alive in this body is a more urgent need for your sake.

Avoid anything in your everyday lives that would be unworthy of the Gospel of Christ. This is the word of the Lord. **Thanks be to God.**

All stand to greet the Gospel. If this Acclamation is not sung it may be omitted.
Alleluia, alleluia! Blessings on the King who comes in the name of the Lord! Peace in heaven and glory in the highest heavens! Alleluia!

or **Alleluia, alleluia! Open our heart, O Lord, to accept the words of your Son. Alleluia!**

GOSPEL   *Matthew 20:1-16*
The Lord be with you. **And also with you.**
A reading from the holy Gospel according to Matthew. **Glory to you, Lord.**

Why be envious because I am generous?

Jesus said to his disciples: "The kingdom of heaven is like a landowner going out at daybreak to hire workers for his vineyard. He made an agreement with the workers for one denarius a day, and sent them to his vineyard. Going out at about the third hour he saw others standing idle in the market place and said to them, 'You go to my vineyard too and I will give you a fair wage.' So they went. At about the sixth hour and again at about the ninth hour, he went out and did the same. Then at about the eleventh hour he went out and found more men standing round, and he said to them, 'Why have you been standing here idle all day?' 'Because no one has hired us,' they answered. He said to them, 'You go into my vineyards too.' In the evening, the owner of the vineyard said to his bailiff, 'Call the workers and pay them their wages, starting with the last arrivals and ending with the first.' So those who were hired at about the eleventh hour came forward and received one denarius each. When the first came, they expected to get more, but they too received one denarius each. They took it, but grumbled at the landowner. 'The men who came last' they said, 'have done only one hour, and you have treated them the same as us, though we have done a heavy day's work in all the heat.' He answered one of them and said, 'My friend, I am not being

unjust to you; did we not agree on one denarius? Take your earnings and go. I choose to pay the last-comer as much as I pay you. Have I no right to do what I like with my own? Why be envious because I am generous?' Thus the last will be first, and the first, last."
This is the Gospel of the Lord. **Praise to you, Lord Jesus Christ.**

The Homily follows, then | *Turn to page 6 for the Creed* |

PRAYER OVER THE GIFTS
Lord,
may these gifts which we now offer
to show our belief and our love
be pleasing to you.
May they become for us
the eucharist of Jesus Christ your Son,
who is Lord for ever and ever.

Turn to pages 8-10 for the Preface and Eucharistic Prayer

COMMUNION ANTIPHON
You have laid down your precepts to be faithfully kept. May my footsteps be firm in keeping your commands.

I am the Good Shepherd, says the Lord; I know my sheep, and mine know me.

PRAYER AFTER COMMUNION
Lord,
help us with your kindness.
Make us strong through the eucharist.
May we put into action
the saving mystery we celebrate.

Turn to page 21 for the Concluding Rite

26th Sunday in Ordinary Time

As the priest goes to the altar everyone joins in this Entrance Antiphon or a hymn.

O Lord, you had just cause to judge men as you did: because we sinned against you and disobeyed your will. But now show us your greatness of heart, and treat us with your unbounded kindness.

Turn to page 4

OPENING PRAYER
Father,
you show your almighty power
in your mercy and forgiveness.
Continue to fill us with your gifts of love.
Help us to hurry toward the eternal life
    you promise
and come to share in the joys of your
    kingdom.

Father of our Lord Jesus Christ,
in your unbounded mercy
you have revealed the beauty of your power
through your constant forgiveness of our sins.
May the power of this love be in our hearts
to bring your pardon and your kingdom
to all we meet.

FIRST READING   A reading from the prophet Ezekiel

When the sinner renounces sin, he shall certainly live.   *Ezekiel 18:25-28*

The word of the Lord was addressed to me as follows: "You object, 'What the Lord does is unjust.' Listen, you House of Israel: is what I do unjust? Is it not what you do that is unjust? When the upright man renounces his integrity to commit sin and dies because of this, he dies because of the evil that he himself has committed. When the sinner renounces sin to become law-abiding and honest, he deserves to live. He has chosen to renounce all his previous sins; he shall certainly live; he shall not die." This is the word of the Lord. **Thanks be to God.**

RESPONSORIAL PSALM   *Psalm 24*
Remember your mercy, Lord.

1. Lord, make me know your ways.
   Lord, teach me your paths.
   Make me walk in your truth, and teach me:
   for you are God my saviour.

2. Remember your mercy, Lord,
   and the love you have shown from of old.
   Do not remember the sins of my youth.
   In your love remember me,
   because of your goodness, O Lord.

3. The Lord is good and upright.
   He shows the path to those who stray,
   he guides the humble in the right path;
   he teaches his way to the poor.

SECOND READING   A reading from the letter of St Paul to the Philippians

In your minds you must be the same as Christ Jesus.   *Philippians 2:1-11 (or 2:1-5)*

If our life in Christ means anything to you, if love can persuade at all, or the Spirit that we have in common, or any tenderness and sympathy, then be united in your convictions and united in your love, with a common purpose and a common mind. That is the one thing which would make me completely happy. There must be no competition among you, no conceit; but everybody is to be self-effacing. Always consider the other person to be better than yourself, so that nobody thinks of his own interests first but everybody thinks of other people's interests instead. In your minds you must be the same as Christ Jesus.
His state was divine, yet he did not cling to his equality with God but emptied himself to assume the condition of a slave, and became as men are; and being as all men are, he was humbler yet, even to accepting death, death on a cross. But God raised him high and gave him the name which is above all other names so that all beings in the heavens, on earth and in the underworld, should bend the knee at the name of Jesus and that every tongue should acclaim Jesus Christ as Lord, to the glory of God the Father.
This is the word of the Lord. **Thanks be to God.**

All stand to greet the Gospel. If this Acclamation is not sung it may be omitted.
Alleluia, alleluia! If anyone loves me he will keep my word, and my Father will love him, and we shall come to him. Alleluia!

or **Alleluia, alleluia! The sheep that belong to me listen to my voice, says the Lord. I know them and they follow me. Alleluia!**

GOSPEL   *Matthew 21:28-32*
The Lord be with you. **And also with you.**
A reading from the holy Gospel according to Matthew. **Glory to you, Lord.**

He thought better of it and went. Tax collectors and prostitutes are making their way into the kingdom of God before you.

Jesus said to the chief priests and the elders of the people, "What is your opinion? A man had two sons. He went and said to the first, 'My boy, you go and work in the vineyard today.' He answered, 'I will not go,' but afterwards thought better of it and went. The man then went and said the same thing to the second who answered, 'Certainly sir,' but did not go. Which of the two did the father's will?" "The first," they said. Jesus said to them, "I tell you solemnly, tax collectors and prostitutes are making their way into the kingdom of God before you. For John came to you, a pattern of true righteousness, but you did not believe him, and yet the tax collectors and prostitutes did. Even after seeing that, you refused to think better of it and believe in him."
This is the Gospel of the Lord. **Praise to you, Lord Jesus Christ.**

The Homily follows then | *Turn to page 6 for the Creed*

PRAYER OVER THE GIFTS
God of mercy,
accept our offering
and make it a source of blessing for us.

Turn to pages 8-10 for the Preface and Eucharistic Prayer

COMMUNION ANTIPHON
O Lord, remember the words you spoke to me, your servant, which made me live in hope and consoled me when I was downcast.

This is how we know what love is: Christ gave up his life for us; and we too must give up our lives for our brothers.

PRAYER AFTER COMMUNION
Lord,
may this eucharist
in which we proclaim the death of Christ
bring us salvation
and make us one with him in glory,
for he is Lord for ever and ever.

Turn to page 21 for the Concluding Rite

27th Sunday in Ordinary Time

As the priest goes to the altar everyone joins in this Entrance Antiphon or a hymn.

O Lord, you have given everything its place in the world, and no one can make it otherwise. For it is your creation, the heavens and the earth and the stars: you are the Lord of all.

Turn to page 4

OPENING PRAYER

Father,
your love for us
surpasses all our hopes and desires.
Forgive our failings,
keep us in your peace
and lead us in the way of salvation.

Almighty and eternal God,
Father of the world to come,
your goodness is beyond what our spirit
can touch
and your strength is more than the mind
can bear.
Lead us to seek beyond our reach
and give us the courage to stand before
your truth.

FIRST READING
A reading from the book of the prophet Isaiah

The vineyard of the Lord of hosts is the House of Israel.
Isaiah 5:1-7

Let me sing to my friend the song of his love for his vineyard. My friend had a vineyard on a fertile hillside. He dug the soil, cleared it of stones, and planted choice vines in it. In the middle he built a tower, he dug a press there too. He expected it to yield grapes, but sour grapes were all that it gave. And now, inhabitants of Jerusalem and men of Judah, I ask you to judge between my vineyard and me. What could I have done for my vineyard that I have not done? I expected it to yield grapes. Why did it yield sour grapes instead? Very well, I will tell you what I am going to do to my vineyard: I will take away its hedge for it to be grazed on, and knock down its wall for it to be trampled on. I will lay it waste, unpruned, undug; overgrown by the briar and the thorn. I will command the clouds to rain no rain on it. Yes, the vineyard of the Lord of hosts is the House of Israel, and the men of Judah that chosen plant. He expected justice, but found bloodshed; integrity, but only a cry of distress.
This is the word of the Lord. **Thanks be to God.**

RESPONSORIAL PSALM
Psalm 79
**The vineyard of the Lord
is the House of Israel.**

1. You brought a vine out of Egypt,
   to plant it you drove out the nations.
   It stretched out its branches to the sea,
   to the Great River it stretched out
   its shoots.

2. Then why have you broken down
   its walls?
   It is plucked by all who pass by.
   It is ravaged by the boar of the forest,
   devoured by the beasts of the field.

3. God of hosts, turn again, we implore,
   look down from heaven and see.
   Visit this vine and protect it,
   the vine your right hand has planted.

4. And we shall never forsake you again:
   give us life that we may call upon
   your name.
   God of hosts, bring us back;
   let your face shine on us and we shall
   be saved.

SECOND READING   A reading from the letter of St Paul to the Philippians
The God of peace will be with you.Philippians 4:6-9

There is no need to worry; but if there is anything you need, pray for it, asking God for it with prayer and thanksgiving, and that peace of God, which is so much greater than we can understand, will guard your hearts and your thoughts, in Christ Jesus. Finally, brothers, fill your minds with everything that is true, everything that is noble, everything that is good and pure, everything that we love and honour, and everything that can be thought virtuous or worthy of praise. Keep doing all the things that you learnt from me and have been taught by me and have heard or seen that I do. Then the God of peace will be with you.
This is the word of the Lord. **Thanks be to God.**

All stand to greet the Gospel. If this Acclamation is not sung it may be omitted.
Alleluia, alleluia! I call you friends, says the Lord, because I have made known to you everything I have learnt from my Father. Alleluia!

or **Alleluia, alleluia! I chose you from the world to go out and bear fruit, fruit that will last, says the Lord. Alleluia!**

GOSPEL   *Matthew 21:33-43*
The Lord be with you. **And also with you.**
A reading from the holy Gospel according to Matthew. **Glory to you, Lord.**
He will lease the vineyard to other tenants.

Jesus said to the chief priests and the elders of the people, "Listen to another parable. There was a man, a landowner, who planted a vineyard; he fenced it round, dug a wine-press in it and built a tower; then he leased it to tenants and went abroad. When vintage time drew near he sent his servants to the tenants to collect his produce. But the tenants seized his servants, thrashed one, killed another and stoned a third. Next he sent some more servants, this time a larger number, and they dealt with them in the same way. Finally he sent his son to them. 'They will respect my son,' he said. But when the tenants saw the son, they said to each other, 'This is the heir. Come on, let us kill him and take over his inheritance.' So they seized him and threw him out of the vineyard and killed him. Now when the owner of the vineyard comes, what will he do to those tenants?" They answered, "He will bring those wretches to a wretched end and lease the vineyard to other tenants who will deliver the produce to him when the season arrives." Jesus said to them, "Have you never read in the scriptures:
It was the stone rejected by the builders that became the keystone. This was the Lord's doing and it is wonderful to see?
"I tell you, then, that the kingdom of God will be taken from you and given to a people who will produce its fruit."
This is the Gospel of the Lord. **Praise to you, Lord Jesus Christ.**

The Homily follows, then Turn to page 6 for the Creed

PRAYER OVER THE GIFTS
Father,
receive these gifts
which our Lord Jesus Christ
has asked us to offer in his memory.
May our obedient service
bring us to the fullness of your redemption.

Turn to pages 8-10 for the Preface and Eucharistic Prayer

COMMUNION ANTIPHON

The Lord is good to those who hope in him, to those who are searching for his love.

Because there is one bread, we, though many, are one body, for we all share in the one loaf and in the one cup.

PRAYER AFTER COMMUNION
Almighty God,
let the eucharist we share
fill us with your life.
May the love of Christ
which we celebrate here
touch our lives and lead us to you.

Turn to page 21 for the Concluding Rite

28th Sunday in Ordinary Time

As the priest goes to the altar everyone joins in this Entrance Antiphon or a hymn.

If you, O Lord, laid bare our guilt, who could endure it? But you are forgiving, God of Israel.

Turn to page 4

OPENING PRAYER
Lord,
our help and guide,
make your love the foundation of our
   lives.
May our love for you express itself
in our eagerness to do good for others.

Father in heaven,
the hand of your loving kindness
powerfully yet gently guides all the
moments of our day.

Go before us in our pilgrimage of life,
anticipate our needs and prevent our
falling.
Send your Spirit to unite us in faith,
that sharing in your service,
we may rejoice in your presence.

FIRST READING   A reading from the prophet Isaiah

The Lord will prepare a banquet, and will wipe away tears from every cheek.

Isaiah 25:6-10

On this mountain, the Lord of hosts will prepare for all peoples a banquet of rich food, a banquet of fine wines, of food rich and juicy, of fine strained wines. On this mountain he will remove the mourning veil covering all peoples, and the shroud enwrapping all nations, he will destroy Death for ever. The Lord will wipe away the tears from every cheek; he will take away his people's shame everywhere on earth, for the Lord has said so. That day, it will be said: See, this is our God in whom we hoped for salvation; the Lord is the one in whom we hoped. We exult and we rejoice that he has saved us; for the hand of the Lord rests on this mountain.
This is the word of the Lord. **Thanks be to God.**

RESPONSORIAL PSALM   *Psalm 22*
**In the Lord's own house shall I dwell
for ever and ever.**

1. The Lord is my shepherd;
   there is nothing I shall want.
   Fresh and green are the pastures
   where he gives me repose.
   Near restful waters he leads me,
   to revive my drooping spirit.

2. He guides me along the right path;
   he is true to his name.
   If I should walk in the valley of
   darkness no evil would I fear.
   You are there with your crook and
   your staff;
   with these you give me comfort.

3. You have prepared a banquet for me
   in the sight of my foes.
   My head you have anointed with oil;
   my cup is overflowing.

4. Surely goodness and kindness shall
   follow me
   all the days of my life.
   In the Lord's house shall I dwell
   for ever and ever.

SECOND READING   A reading from the letter of St Paul to the Philippians
There is nothing I cannot master with the help of the One who gives me strength.
                                            Philippians 4:12-14,19-20

I know how to be poor and I know how to be rich too. I have been through my initiation
and now I am ready for anything anywhere: full stomach or empty stomach, poverty
or plenty. There is nothing I cannot master with the help of the One who gives me
strength. All the same, it was good of you to share with me in my hardships. In return
my God will fulfill all your needs, in Christ Jesus, as lavishly as only God can. Glory
to God, our Father, for ever and ever. Amen.
This is the word of the Lord. **Thanks be to God.**

All stand to greet the Gospel. If this Acclamation is not sung it may be omitted.
**Alleluia, alleluia! The Word was made flesh and lived among us; to all who did accept
him he gave power to become children of God. Alleluia!**

or **Alleluia, alleluia! May the Father of our Lord Jesus Christ enlighten the eyes of
our mind, so that we can see what hope his call holds for us. Alleluia!**

GOSPEL   *Matthew 22:1-14 (or 22:1-10)*
The Lord be with you. **And also with you.**
A reading from the holy Gospel according to Matthew. **Glory to you, Lord.**

Invite everyone you can find to the wedding.

Jesus said to the chief priests and elders of the people: "The kingdom of heaven may
be compared to a king who gave a feast for his son's wedding. He sent his servants to
call those who had been invited, but they would not come. Next he sent some more
servants. 'Tell those who have been invited,' he said, 'that I have my banquet all
prepared, my oxen and fattened cattle have been slaughtered, everything is ready.
Come to the wedding.' But they were not interested: one went off to his farm, another
to his business, and the rest seized his servants, maltreated them and killed them. The
king was furious. He despatched his troops, destroyed those murderers and burnt their
town. Then he said to his servants, 'The wedding is ready; but as those who were
invited proved to be unworthy, go to the crossroads in the town and invite everyone

you can find to the wedding.' So these servants went out on the roads and collected together everyone they could find, bad and good alike; and the wedding hall was filled with guests.

"When the king came in to look at the guests he noticed one man who was not wearing a wedding garment, and said to him, 'How did you get in here, my friend, without a wedding garment?' And the man was silent. Then the king said to the attendants, 'Bind him hand and foot and throw him out into the dark, where there will be weeping and grinding of teeth.' For many are called, but few are chosen."

This is the Gospel of the Lord. **Praise to you, Lord Jesus Christ.**

The Homily follows, then | *Turn to page 6 for the Creed*

PRAYER OVER THE GIFTS
PRAYER OVER THE GIFTS
Lord,
accept the prayers and gifts
we offer in faith and love.
May this eucharist bring us to your glory.

Turn to pages 8-10 for the Preface and Eucharistic Prayer

COMMUNION ANTIPHON
The rich suffer want and go hungry, but nothing shall be lacking to those who fear the Lord.

When the Lord is revealed we shall be like him, for we shall see him as he is.

PRAYER AFTER COMMUNION
Almighty Father,
may the body and blood of your Son
give us a share in his life,
for he is Lord for ever and ever.

Turn to page 21 for the Concluding Rite

29th Sunday in Ordinary Time

As the priest goes to the altar everyone joins in this Entrance Antiphon or a hymn.

I call upon you, God, for you will answer me; bend your ear and hear my prayer. Guard me as the pupil of your eye; hide me in the shade of your wings.

Turn to page 4

OPENING PRAYER
Almighty and ever-living God,
our source of power and inspiration,
give us strength and joy
in serving you as followers of Christ,
who lives and reigns with you and
　　the Holy Spirit,
one God, for ever and ever.

Lord our God, Father of all,
you guard us under the shadow of your wings
and search into the depths of our hearts.

Remove the blindness that cannot know you
and relieve the fear that would hide us from your sight.

FIRST READING A reading from the prophet Isaiah

I have taken Cyrus by his right hand to subdue nations before him. *Isaiah 45:1,4-6*

Thus says the Lord to his anointed, to Cyrus, whom he has taken by his right hand to subdue nations before him and strip the loins of kings, to force gateways before him that their gates be closed no more: It is for the sake of my servant Jacob, of Israel my chosen one, that I have called you by your name, conferring a title though you do not know me. I am the Lord, unrivalled; there is no other God besides me. Though you do not know me, I arm you that men may know from the rising to the setting of the sun that, apart from me, all is nothing.
This is the word of the Lord. **Thanks be to God.**

RESPONSORIAL PSALM *Psalm 95*
Give the Lord glory and power.

1. O sing a new song to the Lord,
   sing to the Lord all the earth.
   Tell among the nations his glory
   and his wonders among all the peoples.

2. The Lord is great and worthy of praise,
   to be feared above all gods;
   the gods of the heathens are naught.
   It was the Lord who made the heavens.

3. Give the Lord, you families of peoples,
   give the Lord glory and power,
   give the Lord the glory of his name.
   Bring an offering and enter his courts.

4. Worship the Lord in his temple.
   O earth, tremble before him.
   Proclaim to the nations: "God is king."
   He will judge the peoples in fairness.

SECOND READING A reading from the first letter of St Paul to the Thessalonians

We constantly remember your faith, your love and your hope. *Thessalonians 1:1-5*

From Paul, Silvanus and Timothy, to the Church in Thessalonika which is in God the Father and the Lord Jesus Christ; wishing you grace and peace from God the Father and the Lord Jesus Christ.
We always mention you in our prayers and thank God for you all, and constantly remember before God our Father how you have shown your faith in action, worked for love and persevered through hope, in our Lord Jesus Christ.
We know, brothers, that God loves you and that you have been chosen, because when we brought the Good News to you, it came to you not only as words, but as power and as the Holy Spirit and as utter conviction.
This is the word of the Lord. **Thanks be to God.**

All stand to greet the Gospel. If this Acclamation is not sung it may be omitted.
Alleluia, alleluia! Your word is truth, O Lord, consecrate us in the truth. Alleluia!

or **Alleluia, alleluia! You will shine in the world like bright stars because you are offering it the word of life. Alleluia!**

GOSPEL *Matthew 22:15-21*
The Lord be with you. **And also with you.**
A reading from the holy Gospel according to Matthew. **Glory to you, Lord.**

Give back to Caesar what belongs to Caesar – and to God what belongs to God.

The Pharisees went away to work out between them how to trap Jesus in what he said. And they sent their disciples to him, together with the Herodians, to say, "Master, we know that you are an honest man and teach the way of God in an honest way, and that you are not afraid of anyone, because a man's rank means nothing to you. Tell us your opinion, then. Is it permissible to pay taxes to Caesar or not?" But Jesus was aware of their malice and replied, "You hypocrites! Why do you set this trap for me? Let me see the money you pay the tax with." They handed him a denarius, and he said, "Whose head is this? Whose name?" "Caesar's," they replied. He then said to them, "Very well, give back to Caesar what belongs to Caesar – and to God what belongs to God." This is the Gospel of the Lord. **Praise to you, Lord Jesus Christ.**

The Homily follows, then   Turn to page 6 for the Creed

PRAYER OVER THE GIFTS
Lord God,
may the gifts we offer
bring us your love and forgiveness
and give us freedom to serve you
    with our lives.

Turn to pages 8-10 for the Preface and Eucharistic Prayer

COMMUNION ANTIPHON
See how the eyes of the Lord are on those who fear him, on those who hope in his love, that he may rescue them from death and feed them in time of famine.

The Son of Man came to give his life as a ransom for many.

PRAYER AFTER COMMUNION
Lord,
may this eucharist help us to remain
    faithful.
May it teach us the way to eternal life.

Turn to page 21 for the Concluding Rite

30th Sunday in Ordinary Time

As the priest goes to the altar everyone joins in this Entrance Antiphon or a hymn.

Let hearts rejoice who search for the Lord. Seek the Lord and his strength, seek always the face of the Lord.

Turn to page 4

OPENING PRAYER
Almighty and ever-living God,
strengthen our faith, hope, and love.
May we do with loving hearts
what you ask of us
and come to share the life you promise.

Praised be you, God and Father of our
Lord Jesus Christ.
There is no power for good
which does not come from your
covenant,
and no promise to hope in
that your love has not offered.
Strengthen our faith to accept your
convenant
and give us the love to carry out your
command.

FIRST READING   A reading from the book of Exodus

If you are harsh with the widow, or with the orphan, my anger will flare against you.

Exodus 22:20-26

The Lord said to Moses, "Tell the sons of Israel this, 'You must not molest the stranger or oppress him, for you lived as strangers in the land of Egypt. You must not be harsh with the widow, or with the orphan; if you are harsh with them, they will surely cry out to me, and be sure I shall hear their cry, my anger will flare and I shall kill you with the sword, your own wives will be widows, your own children orphans.

"If you lend money to any of my people, to any poor man among you, you must not play the usurer with him; you must not demand interest from him.

"If you take another's cloak as a pledge, you must give it back to him before sunset. It is all the covering he has; it is the cloak he wraps his body in; what else would he sleep in? If he cries to me, I will listen, for I am full of pity.' "

This is the word of the Lord. **Thanks be to God.**

RESPONSORIAL PSALM   *Psalm 17*
I love you, Lord, my strength.

1. I love you, Lord, my strength,
   my rock, my fortress, my saviour.
   My God is the rock where I take refuge;
   my shield, my mighty help,
      my stronghold.
   The Lord is worthy of all praise:
   when I call I am saved from my foes.

2. Long life to the Lord, my rock!
   Praised be the God who saves me.
   He has given great victories to his king
   and shown his love for his anointed.

SECOND READING   A reading from the first letter of St Paul to the Thessalonians

You broke with idolatry and became servants of God; you are now waiting for his Son.

1 Thessalonians 1:5-10

You observed the sort of life we lived when we were with you, which was for your instruction, and you were led to become imitators of us, and the Lord; and it was with the joy of the Holy Spirit that you took to the Gospel, in spite of the great opposition all round you. This has made you the great example to all believers in Macedonia and Achaia since it was from you that the word of the Lord started to spread – and not only throughout Macedonia and Achaia, for the news of your faith in God has spread everywhere. We do not need to tell other people about it; other people tell us how we started the work among you, how you broke with idolatry when you were converted to God and became servants of the real, living God; and how you are now waiting for Jesus, his Son, whom he raised from the dead, to come from heaven to save us from the retribution which is coming.

This is the word of the Lord. **Thanks be to God.**

All stand to greet the Gospel. If this Acclamation is not sung it may be omitted.
Alleluia, alleluia! Open our heart, O Lord, to accept the words of your Son. Alleluia!

or **Alleluia, alleluia! If anyone loves me he will keep my word, and my Father will love him, and we shall come to him. Alleluia!**

GOSPEL   *Mathew 22:34-40*
The Lord be with you. **And also with you.**
A reading from the holy Gospel according to Matthew. **Glory to you, Lord.**

You must love the Lord your God and your neighbour as yourself.

When the Pharisees heard that Jesus had silenced the Sadducees they got together and, to disconcert him, one of them put a question, "Master, which is the greatest commandment of the Law?" Jesus said, "You must love the Lord your God with all your heart, with all your soul, and with all your mind. This is the greatest and the first commandment. The second resembles it: You must love your neighbour as yourself. On these two commandments hang the whole Law, and the Prophets also."
This is the Gospel of the Lord. **Praise to you, Lord Jesus Christ.**

The Homily follows, then | Turn to page 6 for the Creed. |

PRAYER OVER THE GIFTS
Lord God of power and might,
receive the gifts we offer
and let our service give you glory.

| *Turn to pages 8-10 for the Preface and Eucharistic Prayer* |

COMMUNION ANTIPHON
We will rejoice at the victory of God and   Christ loved us and gave himself up for
make our boast in his great name.   us a fragrant offering to God.

PRAYER AFTER COMMUNION
Lord,
bring to perfection within us
the communion we share in this sacrament,
may our celebration have an effect
   in our lives. | *Turn to page 21 for the Concluding Rite* |

31st Sunday in Ordinary Time

As the priest goes to the altar everyone joins in this Entrance Antiphon or a hymn.
Do not abandon me, Lord. My God, do not go away from me! Hurry to help me, Lord, my Saviour. | *Turn to page 4* |

OPENING PRAYER
God of power and mercy,
only with your help
can we offer you fitting service
   and praise.
May we live the faith we profess
and trust your promise of eternal
life.

Father in heaven, God of power and Lord of
mercy,
from whose fullness we have received,
direct our steps in our everyday efforts.
May the changing moods of the human heart
and the limits which our failings impose on hope
never blind us to you, source of every good.

Faith gives us the promise of peace
and makes known the demands of love.
Remove the selfishness that blurs the vision of
faith.

FIRST READING   A reading from the prophet Malachi

You have strayed from the way; you have caused many to stumble by your teaching.
Malachi 1:14-2:2,8-10

I am a great king, says the Lord of hosts, and my name is feared throughout the nations.
And now, priests, this warning is for you. If you do not listen, if you do not find it in
your heart to glorify my name, says the Lord of hosts, I will send the curse on you and
curse your very blessing. You have strayed from the way; you have caused many to
stumble by your teaching. You have destroyed the covenant of Levi, says the Lord of
hosts. And so I in my turn have made you contemptible and vile in the eyes of the
whole people in repayment for the way you have not kept to my paths but have shown
partiality in your administration.
Have we not all one Father? Did not one God create us? Why, then, do we break faith
with one another, profaning the covenant of our ancestors?
This is the word of the Lord. **Thanks be to God.**

RESPONSORIAL PSALM   *Psalm 130*
Keep my soul in peace before you, O Lord.

1. O Lord, my heart is not proud
   nor haughty my eyes.
   I have not gone after things too great
   nor marvels beyond me.

2. Truly I have set my soul
   in silence and peace.
   A weaned child on its mother's breast,
   even so is my soul.

3. O Israel, hope in the Lord
   both now and for ever.

SECOND READING   A reading from the first letter of St Paul to the Thessalonians

We were eager to hand over to you not only the Good News but our whole lives as well.
1 Thessalonians 2:7-9,13

Like a mother feeding and looking after her own children, we felt so devoted and
protective towards you, and had come to love you so much, that we were eager to
hand over to you not only the Good News but our whole lives as well. Let me remind
you, brothers, how hard we used to work, slaving night and day so as not to be a
burden on any one of you while we were proclaiming God's Good News to you.
Another reason why we constantly thank God for you is that as soon as you heard the
message that we brought you as God's message, you accepted it for what it really is,
God's message and not some human thinking; and it is still a living power among you
who believe it.
This is the word of the Lord. **Thanks be to God.**

All stand to greet the Gospel. If this Acclamation is not sung it may be omitted.
**Alleluia, alleluia! Speak, Lord, your servant is listening: you have the message of
eternal life. Alleluia!**

or **Alleluia, alleluia! You have only one Father, and he is in heaven; you have only
one Teacher, the Christ! Alleluia!**

GOSPEL *Matthew 23:1-12*
The Lord be with you. **And also with you.**
A reading from the holy Gospel according to Matthew. **Glory to you, Lord.**

They do not practise what they preach.

Addressing the people and his disciples Jesus said, "The scribes and the Pharisees occupy the chair of Moses. You must therefore do what they tell you and listen to what they say; but do not be guided by what they do: since they do not practise what they preach. They tie up heavy burdens and lay them on men's shoulders, but will they lift a finger to move them? Not they! Everything they do is done to attract attention, like wearing broader phylacteries and longer tassels, like wanting to take the place of honour at banquets and the front seats in the synagogues, being greeted obsequiously in the market squares and having people call them Rabbi.

"You, however, must not allow yourselves to be called Rabbi, since you have only one Master, and you are all brothers. You must call no one on earth your father, since you have only one Father, and he is in heaven. Nor must you allow yourselves to be called teachers, for you have only one Teacher, the Christ. The greatest among you must be your servant. Anyone who exalts himself will be humbled, and anyone who humbles himself will be exalted."
This is the Gospel of the Lord. **Praise to you, Lord Jesus Christ.**

The Homily follows, then | Turn to page 6 for the Creed |

PRAYER OVER THE GIFTS
God of mercy,
may we offer a pure sacrifice
for the forgiveness of our sins.

| *Turn to pages 8-10 for the Preface and Eucharistic Prayer* |

COMMUNION ANTIPHON
Lord, you will show me the path of life and fill me with joy in your presence.

As the living Father sent me, and I live because of the Father, so he who eats my flesh and drinks my blood will live because of me.

PRAYER AFTER COMMUNION
Lord,
you give us new hope in this eucharist.
May the power of your love
continue its saving work among us
and bring us to the joy you promise.

| *Turn to page 21 for the Concluding Rite* |

32nd Sunday in Ordinary Time

As the priest goes to the altar everyone joins in this Entrance Antiphon or a hymn.
Let my prayer come before you, Lord; listen, and answer me.

Turn to page 4

OPENING PRAYER

God of power and mercy,
protect us from all harm.
Give us freedom of spirit
and health in mind and body
to do your work on earth.

Almighty Father,
strong is your justice and great is your mercy.
Protect us in the burdens and challenges of life.
Shield our minds from the distortion of pride
and enfold our desire with the beauty of truth.

Help us to become more aware of your loving design
so that we may more willingly give our lives in service
to all.

FIRST READING   A reading from the book of Wisdom

Wisdom is found by those who look for her.   *Wisdom 6:12-16*

Wisdom is bright, and does not grow dim. By those who love her she is readily seen,
and found by those who look for her. Quick to anticipate those who desire her, she
makes herself known to them. Watch for her early and you will have no trouble; you
will find her sitting at your gates. Even to think about her is understanding fully grown;
be on the alert for her and anxiety will quickly leave you. She herself walks about
looking for those who are worthy of her and graciously shows herself to them as they
go, in every thought of theirs coming to meet them.
This is the word of the Lord. **Thanks be to God.**

RESPONSORIAL PSALM   *Psalm 62*
For you my soul is thirsting, O God, my God.

1. O God, you are my God, for you I long;
   for you my soul is thirsting.
   My body pines for you
   like a dry, weary land without water.

2. So I gaze on you in the sanctuary
   to see your strength and your glory.
   For your love is better than life,
   my lips will speak your praise.

3. So I will bless you all my life,
   in your name I will lift up my hands.
   My soul shall be filled as with a banquet,
   my mouth shall praise you with joy.

4. On my bed, I remember you.
   On you I muse through the night
   for you have been my help;
   in the shadow of your wings I rejoice.

SECOND READING   A reading from the first letter of St Paul to the Thessalonians

God will bring with him those who have died in Jesus.

1 Thessalonians 4:13-18 (or 4:13-14)

We want you to be quite certain, brothers, about those who have died, to make sure
that you do not grieve about them, like the other people who have no hope. We believe
that Jesus died and rose again, and that it will be the same for those who have died in
Jesus: God will bring them with him.
We can tell you this from the Lord's own teaching, that any of us who are left alive
until the Lord's coming will not have any advantage over those who have died. At the
trumpet of God, the voice of the archangel will call out the command and the Lord

himself will come down from heaven; those who have died in Christ will be the first to rise, and then those of us who are still alive will be taken up in the clouds, together with them, to meet the Lord in the air. So we shall stay with the Lord for ever. With such thoughts as these you should comfort one another.
This is the word of the Lord. **Thanks be to God.**

All stand to greet the Gospel. If this Acclamation is not sung it may be omitted.
Alleluia, alleluia! Stay awake and stand ready, because you do not know the hour when the Son of Man is coming. Alleluia!

GOSPEL   *Matthew 25:1-13*
The Lord be with you. **And also with you.**
A reading from the holy Gospel according to Matthew. **Glory to you, Lord.**
The bridegroom is here! Go out and meet him.

Jesus told this parable to his disciples: "The kingdom of heaven will be like this: Ten bridesmaids took their lamps and went to meet the bridegroom. Five of them were foolish and five were sensible: the foolish ones did take their lamps, but they brought no oil, whereas the sensible ones took flasks of oil as well as their lamps. The bridegroom was late, and they all grew drowsy and fell asleep. But at midnight there was a cry, 'The bridegroom is here! Go out and meet him.' At this, all those bridesmaids woke up and trimmed their lamps, and the foolish ones said to the sensible ones, 'Give us some of your oil: our lamps are going out.' But they replied, 'There may not be enough for us and for you; you had better go to those who sell it and buy some for yourselves.' They had gone off to buy it when the bridegroom arrived. Those who were ready went in with him to the wedding hall and the door was closed. The other bridesmaids arrived later. 'Lord, Lord,' they said 'open the door for us.' But he replied, 'I tell you solemnly, I do not know you.' So stay awake, because you do not know either the day or the hour."
This is the Gospel of the Lord. **Praise to you, Lord Jesus Christ.**

The Homily follows, then   Turn to page 6 for the Creed

PRAYER OVER THE GIFTS
God of mercy,
in this eucharist we proclaim the death
    of the Lord.
Accept the gifts we present
and help us follow him with love,   *Turn to pages 8-10 for the Preface and Eucharistic Prayer*
for he is Lord for ever and ever.

COMMUNION ANTIPHON
The Lord is my shepherd; there is nothing I shall want. In green pastures he gives me rest, he leads me beside the waters of peace.

The disciples recognised the Lord Jesus in the breaking of the bread.

PRAYER AFTER COMMUNION
Lord,
we thank you for the nourishment you give us
through your holy gift.
Pour out your Spirit upon us
and in the strength of this food from heaven
keep us single-minded in your service.

Turn to page 21 for
the Concluding Rite

33rd Sunday in Ordinary Time

As the priest goes to the altar everyone joins in this Entrance Antiphon or a hymn.
The Lord says: my plans for you are peace and not disaster; when you call to me, I will listen to you, and I will bring you back to the place from which I exiled you.

Turn to page 4

OPENING PRAYER
Father of all that is good,
keep us faithful in serving you,
for to serve you is our lasting joy.

Father in heaven,
ever-living source of all that is good,
from the beginning of time you promised man
salvation
through the future coming of your Son, our
Lord Jesus Christ.

Help us to drink of his truth
and expand our hearts with the joy of his
promises,
so that we may serve you in faith and in love
and know for ever the joy of your presence.

FIRST READING   A reading from the book of Proverbs

A perfect wife – who can find her?   *Proverbs 31:10-13,19-20,30-31*

A perfect wife – who can find her? She is far beyond the price of pearls. Her husband's heart has confidence in her, from her he will derive no little profit. Advantage and not hurt she brings him all the days of her life. She is always busy with wool and with flax, she does her work with eager hands. She sets her hand to the distaff, her fingers grasp the spindle. She holds out her hand to the poor, she opens her arms to the needy. Charm is deceitful, and beauty empty; the woman who is wise is the one to praise. Give her a share in what her hands have worked for, and let her works tell her praises at the city gates.
This is the word of the Lord. **Thanks be to God.**

RESPONSORIAL PSALM   *Psalm 127*
O blessed are those who fear the Lord.

1. O blessed are those who fear the Lord
   and walk in his ways!
   By the labour of your hands you shall eat.
   You will be happy and prosper.

2. Your wife like a fruitful vine
   in the heart of your house;
   your children like shoots of the olive,
   around your table.

3. Indeed thus shall be blessed
the man who fears the Lord.
May the Lord bless you from Zion
in a happy Jerusalem
all the days of your life.

SECOND READING   A reading from the first letter of St Paul to the Thessalonians

Let not the Day of the Lord overtake you like a thief.   *1 Thessalonians 5:1-6*

You will not be expecting us to write anything to you, brothers, about "times and seasons", since you know very well that the Day of the Lord is going to come like a thief in the night. It is when people are saying, "How quiet and peaceful it is" that the worst suddenly happens, as suddenly as labour pains come on a pregnant woman; and there will be no way for anybody to evade it.
But it is not as if you live in the dark, my brothers, for that Day to overtake you like a thief. No, you are all sons of light and sons of the day; we do not belong to the night or to darkness, so we should not go on sleeping, as everyone else does, but stay wide awake and sober.
This is the word of the Lord. **Thanks be to God.**

All stand to greet the Gospel. If this Acclamation is not sung it may be omitted.
Alleluia, alleluia! Even if you have to die, says the Lord, keep faithful, and I will give you the crown of life. Alleluia!

or **Alleluia, alleluia! Make your home in me, as I make mine in you, says the Lord. Whoever remains in me bears fruit in plenty. Alleluia!**

GOSPEL   *Matthew 25:14-30 (or 25:14-15,19-21)*
The Lord be with you. **And also with you.**
A reading from the holy Gospel according to Matthew. **Glory to you, Lord.**

You have been faithful in small things; come and join in your master's happiness.

Jesus spoke this parable to his disciples: "The kingdom of heaven is like a man on his way abroad who summoned his servants and entrusted his property to them. To one he gave five talents, to another two, to a third one; each in proportion to his ability. Then he set out.
"The man who had received the five talents promptly went and traded with them and made five more. The man who had received two made two more in the same way. But the man who had received one went off and dug a hole in the ground and hid his master's money.
"Now a long time after, the master of those servants came back and went through his accounts with them. The man who had received the five talents came forward bringing five more. 'Sir', he said, 'you entrusted me with five talents; here are five more that I have made.'
"His master said to him, 'Well done, good and faithful servant; you have shown you can be faithful in small things, I will trust you with greater; come and join in your master's happiness.' Next the man with two talents came forward. 'Sir', he said, 'you entrusted me with two talents; here are two more that I have made.' His master said to him, 'Well done, good and faithful servant; you have shown you can be faithful in small things, I will trust you with greater; come and join in your master's happiness.' Last came forward the man who had one talent. 'Sir', said he, 'I had heard you were

a hard man, reaping where you have not sown and gathering where you have not scattered; so I was afraid, and I went off and hid your talent in the ground. Here it is; it was yours, you have it back.' But his master answered him, 'You wicked and lazy servant! So you knew that I reap where I have not sown and gather where I have not scattered? Well then, you should have deposited my money with the bankers, and on my return I would have recovered iny capital with interest. So now, take the talent from him and give it to the man who has the five talents. For everyone who has will be given more, and he will have more than enough; but from the man who has not, even what he has will be taken away. As for this good-for-nothing servant, throw him out into the dark, where there will be weeping and grinding of teeth.' "
This is the Gospel of the Lord. **Praise to you, Lord Jesus Christ.**

The Homily follows, then Turn to page 6 for the Creed

PRAYER OVER THE GIFTS
Lord God,
may the gifts we offer
increase our love for you
and bring us to eternal life.

*Turn to pages 8-10 for the
Preface and Eucharistic Prayer*

COMMUNION ANTIPHON
It is good for me to be with the Lord and to put my hope in him.

I tell you solemnly, whatever you ask for in prayer, believe that you have received it, and it will be yours, says the Lord.

PRAYER AFTER COMMUNION
Father,
may we grow in love
by the eucharist we have celebrated
in memory of the Lord Jesus,
who is Lord for ever and ever.

Turn to page 21 for the Concluding Rite

LAST SUNDAY OF THE YEAR
Our Lord Jesus Christ, Universal King

As the priest goes to the altar everyone joins in this Entrance Antiphon or a hymn.
The Lamb who was slain is worthy to receive strength and divinity, wisdom and power and honour: to him be glory and power for ever.

Turn to page 4

OPENING PRAYER

Almighty and merciful God,
you break the power of evil
and make all things new
in your Son Jesus Christ, the King of
the universe.
May all in heaven and earth acclaim
your glory
and never cease to praise you.

Father all-powerful, God of love,
you have raised our Lord Jesus Christ from
death to life,
resplendent in glory as King of creation.
Open our hearts,
free all the world to rejoice in his peace,
to glory in his justice, to live in his love.
Bring all mankind together in Jesus Christ
your Son,
whose kingdom is with you and the Holy
Spirit, one God, for ever and ever.

FIRST READING   A reading from the prophet Ezekiel
As for you, my sheep, I will judge between sheep and sheep.   *Ezekiel 34:11-12,15-17*

The Lord says this: I am going to look after my flock myself and keep all of it in view.
As a shepherd keeps all his flock in view when he stands up in the middle of his
scattered sheep, so shall I keep my sheep in view. I shall rescue them from wherever
they have been scattered during the mist and darkness. I myself will pasture my sheep,
I myself will show them where to rest – it is the Lord who speaks. I shall look for the
lost one, bring back the stray, bandage the wounded and make the weak strong. I shall
watch over the fat and healthy. I shall be a true shepherd to them.
As for you, my sheep, the Lord says this: I will judge between sheep and sheep, between
rams and he-goats.   This is the word of the Lord. **Thanks be to God.**

RESPONSORIAL PSALM   *Psalm 22*
The Lord is my shepherd; there is nothing I shall want.

1. The Lord is my shepherd;
   there is nothing I shall want.
   Fresh and green are the pastures
   where he gives me repose.

2. Near restful waters he leads me,
   to revive my drooping spirit.
   He guides me along the right path;
   he is true to his name.

3. You have prepared a banquet for me
   in the sight of my foes.
   My head you have anointed with oil;
   my cup overflowing.

4. Surely goodness and kindness shall
   follow me all the days of my life.
   In the Lord's own house shall I dwell
   for ever and ever.

SECOND READING   A reading from the first letter of St Paul to the Corinthians
He will hand over the kingdom to God the Father, so that God may be all in all.
                                        1 Corinthians 15:20-26,28

Christ has been raised from the dead, the first-fruits of all who have fallen asleep.
Death came through one man and in the same way the resurrection of the dead has
come through one man. Just as all men die in Adam, so all men will be brought to life
in Christ; but all of them in their proper order: Christ as the first-fruits and then, after
the coming of Christ, those who belong to him. After that will come the end, when he
hands over the kingdom to God the Father, having done away with every sovereignty,
authority and power. For he must be king until he has put all his enemies under his
feet and the last of the enemies to be destroyed is death. And when everything is
subjected to him, then the Son himself will be subject in his turn to the One who
subjected all things to him, so that God may be all in all.
This is the word of the Lord. **Thanks be to God.**

All stand to greet the Gospel. If this Acclamation is not sung it may be omitted.
Alleluia, alleluia! Blessings on him who comes in the name of the Lord! Blessings on the coming kingdom of our father David! Alleluia!

GOSPEL   *Matthew 25:31-46*
The Lord be with you. **And also with you.**
A reading from the holy Gospel according to Matthew. **Glory to you, Lord.**

He will take his seat on his throne of glory, and he will separate men one from another.

Jesus said to his disciples: "When the Son of Man comes in his glory, escorted by all the angels, then he will take his seat on his throne of glory. All the nations will be assembled before him and he will separate men one from another as the shepherd separates sheep from goats. He will place the sheep on his right hand and the goats on his left. Then the King will say to those on his right hand. 'Come you whom my Father has blessed, take for your heritage the kingdom prepared for you since the foundation of the world. For I was hungry and you gave me food; I was thirsty and you gave me drink; I was a stranger and you made me welcome; naked and you clothed me, sick and you visited me, in prison and you came to see me.' Then the virtuous will say to him in reply, 'Lord, when did we see you hungry and feed you; or thirsty and give you drink? When did we see you a stranger and make you welcome; naked and clothed you; sick or in prison and go to see you?' And the King will answer, 'I tell you solemnly, in so far as you did this to one of the least of these brothers of mine, you did it to me.' Next he will say to those on his left hand, 'Go away from me, with your curse upon you, to the eternal fire prepared for the devil and his angels. For I was hungry and you never gave me food; I was thirsty and you never gave me anything to drink; I was a stranger and you never made me welcome, naked and you never clothed me, sick and in prison and you never visited me.' Then it will be their turn to ask, 'Lord, when did we see you hungry or thirsty, a stranger or naked, sick or in prison, and did not come to your help?' Then he will answer, 'I tell you solemnly, in so far as you neglected to do this to one of the least of these, you neglected to do it to me.' And they will go away to eternal punishment, and the virtuous to eternal life."
This is the Gospel of the Lord. **Praise to you, Lord Jesus Christ.**

The Homily follows, then Turn to page 6 for the Creed

PRAYER OVER THE GIFTS
Lord,
we offer you the sacrifice
by which your Son reconciles mankind.
May it bring unity and peace to the world.

PREFACE OF CHRIST THE KING
The Lord be with you.   **And also with you.**
Lift up your hearts.   **We lift them up to the Lord.**
Let us give thanks to the Lord our God.   **It is right to give him thanks and praise.**

Father, all-powerful and ever-living God,
we do well always and everywhere to give you thanks.
You anointed Jesus Christ, your only Son, with the oil of gladness,
as the eternal priest and universal King.

As priest he offered his life on the altar of the cross
and redeemed the human race
by this one perfect sacrifice of peace.

As King he claims dominion over all creation,
that he may present to you, his almighty Father,
an eternal and universal kingdom:
a kingdom of truth and life,
a kingdom of holiness and grace,
a kingdom of justice, love, and peace.

And so, with all the choirs of angels in heaven
we proclaim your glory
and join in their unending hymn of praise:

**Holy, holy, holy Lord, God of power and might,
heaven and earth are full of your glory.
Hosanna in the highest.**

**Blessed is he who comes in the name of the Lord.
Hosanna in the highest.**

*Turn to
page 10 for Eucharistic Prayer 1
page 13 for Eucharistic Prayer 2
page 15 for Eucharistic Prayer 3*

COMMUNION ANTIPHON
The Lord will reign for ever and will give his people the gift of peace.

PRAYER AFTER COMMUNION
Lord,
you give us Christ, the King of all
    creation,
as food for everlasting life.
Help us to live by his Gospel
and bring us to the joy of his kingdom,
where he lives and reigns for ever and
    ever.

Turn to page 21 for the Concluding Rite

JUNE 24TH

The Birth of St John the Baptist

(The Mass for the Vigil is on p.123)
As the priest goes to the altar everyone joins in this Entrance Antiphon or a hymn.

**There was a man sent from God whose name was John. He came to bear witness
to the light, to prepare an upright people for the Lord.**

Turn to page 4

OPENING PRAYER

God our Father,
you raised up John the Baptist
to prepare a perfect people for Christ
    the Lord.
Give your Church joy in spirit
and guide those who believe in you
into the way of salvation and peace.

God our Father,
the voice of John the Baptist challenges
    us to repentance
and points the way to Christ the Lord.
Open our ears to his message, and free
    our hearts
to turn from our sins and receive the life
    of the gospel.

FIRST READING   A reading from the Prophet Isaiah

I will make you the light of the nations.   *Isaiah 49:1-6*

Islands, listen to me, pay attention remotest peoples. The Lord called me before I was born, from my mother's womb he pronounced my name.
He made my mouth a sharp sword, and hid me in the shadow of his hand. He made me into a sharpened arrow, and concealed me in his quiver.
He said to me, "You are my servant (Israel) in whom I shall be glorified": while I was thinking, "I have toiled in vain, I have exhausted myself for nothing": and all the while my cause was with the Lord, my reward with my God. I was honoured in the eyes of the Lord, my God was my strength.
And now the Lord has spoken, he who formed me in the womb to be his servant, to bring Jacob back to him, to gather Israel to him:
"It is not enough for you to be my servant, to restore the tribes of Jacob and bring back the survivors of Israel; I will make you the light of the nations so that my salvation may reach to the ends of the earth."
This is the word of the Lord. **Thanks be to God.**

RESPONSORIAL PSALM   *Psalm 138*
I thank you for the wonder of my being.

1. O Lord, you search me and you
        know me,
    you know my resting and my rising,
    you discern my purpose from afar.
    You mark when I walk or lie down,
    all my ways lie open to you.

2. For it was you who created my being,
    knit me together in my mother's womb.
    I thank you for the wonder of my being,
    for the wonders of all your creation.

3. Already you knew my soul,
    my body held no secret from you
    when I was being fashioned in secret
    and moulded in the depths of the earth.

SECOND READING   A reading from the Acts of the Apostles

Jesus, whose coming was heralded by John.   *Acts 13:22-26*

Paul said: "God made David the king of our ancestors, of whom he approved in these words, 'I have selected David son of Jesse, a man after my own heart, who will carry out my whole purpose.' To keep his promise, God has raised up for Israel one of David's descendants, Jesus, as Saviour, whose coming was heralded by John when he proclaimed a baptism of repentance for the whole people of Israel. Before John ended his career he said, 'I am not the one you imagine me to be; that one is coming after me and I am not fit to undo his sandal.'

"My brothers, sons of Abraham's race, and all you who fear God, this message of salvation is meant for you."
This is the word of the Lord. **Thanks be to God.**

All stand to greet the Gospel. If this Acclamation is not sung it may be omitted.
Alleluia, alleluia! As for you, little child, you shall be called a prophet of God, the Most High. You shall go ahead of the Lord to prepare his ways before him. Alleluia!

THE GOSPEL   *Luke 1:57-66,80*
The Lord be with you. **And also with you.**
A reading from the holy Gospel according to Luke. **Glory to you, Lord.**

His name is John.

The time came for Elizabeth to have her child, and she gave birth to a son; and when her neighbours and relations heard that the Lord had shown her so great a kindness, they shared her joy.
Now on the eighth day they came to circumcise the child; they were going to call him Zechariah after his father, but his mother spoke up. "No," she said "he is to be called John." They said to her, "But no one in your family has that name", and made signs to his father to find out what he wanted him called. The father asked for a writing tablet and wrote, "His name is John." And they were all astonished. At that instant his power of speech returned and he spoke and praised God. All their neighbours were filled with awe and the whole affair was talked about throughout the hill country of Judaea. All those who heard of it treasured it in their hearts. "What will this child turn out to be?" they wondered. And indeed the hand of the Lord was with him. The child grew up and his spirit matured. And he lived out in the wilderness until the day he appeared openly to Israel.
This is the Gospel of the Lord. **Praise to you, Lord Jesus Christ.**

The Homily follows, then   Turn to page 6 for the Creed

PRAYER OVER THE GIFTS
Father,
accept the gifts we bring to your altar to
celebrate the birth of John the Baptist,
who foretold the coming of our Saviour
and made him known when he came.

PREFACE OF ST JOHN THE BAPTIST
The Lord be with you.   **And also with you.**
Lift up your hearts.   **We lift them up to the Lord.**
Let us give thanks to the Lord our God. **It is right to give him thanks and praise.**

Father, all-powerful and ever-living God,
we do well always and everywhere to give you thanks
through Jesus Christ our Lord.

We praise your greatness
as we honour the prophet
who prepared the way before your Son.
You set John the Baptist apart from other men,
marking him out with special favour.

His birth brought great rejoicing:
even in the womb he leapt for joy,
so near was man's salvation.

You chose John the Baptist from all the prophets
to show the world its Redeemer,
the lamb of sacrifice.
He baptised Christ, the giver of baptism,
in waters made holy by the one who was baptised.
You found John worthy of a martyr's death,
his last and greatest act of witness to your Son.

In our unending joy we echo on earth
the song of the angels in heaven
as they praise your glory for ever:
**Holy, holy, holy Lord, God of power and might,
heaven and earth are full of your glory.
   Hosanna in the highest.**

**Blessed is he who comes in the name of the Lord.
   Hosanna in the highest.**

*Turn to
page 10 for Eucharistic Prayer 1
page 13 for Eucharistic Prayer 2
page 15 for Eucharistic Prayer 3*

COMMUNION ANTIPHON
Through the tender compassion of our God, the dawn from on high shall break upon us.

PRAYER AFTER COMMUNION
Lord,
you have renewed us with this eucharist,
as we celebrate the feast of John
   the Baptist,
who foretold the coming of the Lamb
   of God.
May we welcome your Son as
   our Saviour,
for he gives us new life,
and is Lord for ever and ever.

Turn to page 21 for the Concluding Rite

JUNE 29TH

Ss Peter and Paul, Apostles

(The Mass for the Vigil is on p.126)
As the priest goes to the altar everyone joins in this Entrance Antiphon or a hymn.

These men, conquering all human frailty, shed their blood and helped the Church to grow. By sharing the cup of the Lord's suffering, they became the friends of God.

Turn to page 4

OPENING PRAYER

God our Father,
today you give us the joy
of celebrating the feast of the
   apostles Peter and Paul.
Through them your Church
   first received the faith.
Keep us true to their teaching.

Praise to you, the God and Father of our
   Lord Jesus Christ,
who in your great mercy have given us new birth
and hope through the power of Christ's
   resurrection.
Through the prayers of the apostles Peter and Paul
may we who receive this faith through their
   preaching
share their joy in following the Lord to the
   unfading inheritance reserved for use in heaven.

FIRST READING   A reading from the Acts of the Apostles
Now I know the Lord really did save me from Herod.   *Acts 12:1-11*

King Herod started persecuting members of the Church. He beheaded James the brother
of John, and when he saw that this pleased the Jews he decided to arrest Peter as well.
This was during the days of Unleavened Bread, and he put Peter in prison, assigning
four squads of four soldiers each to guard him in turns. Herod meant to try Peter in
public after the end of the Passover week. All the time Peter was under guard the
Church prayed to God for him unremittingly.
On the night before Herod was to try him, Peter was sleeping between two soldiers,
fastened with double chains, while guards kept watch at the main entrance to the
prison. Then suddenly the angel of the Lord stood there, and the cell was filled with
light. He tapped Peter on the side and woke him. "Get up!" he said "Hurry!" – and the
chains fell from his hands. The angel then said, "Put on your belt and sandals." After
he had done this, the angel next said, "Wrap your cloak round you and follow me."
Peter followed him, but had no idea that what the angel did was happening in reality;
he thought he was seeing a vision. They passed through two guard posts one after the
other, and reached the iron gate leading to the city. This opened of its own accord;
they went through it and had walked the whole length of one street when suddenly the
angel left him. It was only then that Peter came to himself. "Now I know it is all true,"
he said. "The Lord really did send his angel and has saved me from Herod and from
all that the Jewish people were so certain would happen to me."
This is the word of the Lord. **Thanks be to God.**

RESPONSORIAL PSALM   *Psalm 33*
From all my terrors the Lord set me free.
or **The angel of the Lord rescues those who revere him.**

1. I will bless the Lord at all times,
   his praise always on my lips;
   in the Lord my soul shall make its boast.
   The humble shall hear and be glad.

2. Glorify the Lord with me.
   Together let us praise his name.
   I sought the Lord and he answered me;
   from all my terrors he set me free.

3. Look towards him and be radiant;
   let your faces not be at ashed.
   This poor man called; the Lord heard him
   and rescued him from all his distress.

4. The angel of the Lord is encamped
   around those who revere him,
      to rescue them.
   Taste and see that the Lord is good.
   He is happy who seeks refuge in him.

SECOND READING   A reading from the second letter of St Paul to Timothy
All there is to come now is the crown of righteousness reserved for me. 2 Timothy 4:6-8,17-18

My life is already being poured away as a libation, and the time has come for me to be gone. I have fought the good fight to the end; I have run the race to the finish; I have kept the faith; all there is to come now is the crown of righteousness reserved for me, which the Lord, the righteous judge, will give to me on that Day; and not only to me but to all those who have longed for his Appearing.
The Lord stood by me and gave me power, so that through me the whole message might be proclaimed for all the pagans to hear; and so I was rescued from the lion's mouth. The Lord will rescue me from all evil attempts on me, and bring me safely to his heavenly kingdom. To him be glory for ever and ever. Amen.
This is the word of the Lord. **Thanks be to God.**

All stand to greet the Gospel. If this Acclamation is not sung it may be omitted.
Alleluia, alleluia! You are Peter and on this rock I will build my Church. And the gates of the underworld can never hold out against it. Alleluia!

THE GOSPEL   *Matthew 16:13-19*
The Lord be with you. **And also with you.**
A reading from the holy Gospel according to Matthew. **Glory to you, Lord.**
You are Peter, and I will give you the keys of the kingdom of heaven.

When Jesus came to the region of Caesarea Philippi he put this question to his disciples, "Who do people say the Son of Man is?"And they said, "Some say he is John the Baptist, some Elijah, and others Jeremiah or one of the prophets." "But you," he said, "who do you say I am?" Then Simon Peter spoke up. "You are the Christ," he said "the Son of the living God." Jesus replied, "Simon son of Jonah, you are a happy man! Because it was not flesh and blood that revealed this to you but my Father in heaven. So I now say to you: You are Peter and on this rock I will build my Church. And the gates of the underworld can never hold out against it. I will give you the keys of the kingdom of heaven: whatever you bind on earth shall be considered bound in heaven; whatever you loose on earth shall be considered loosed in heaven."
This is the Gospel of the Lord. **Praise to you, Lord Jesus Christ.**

The Homily follows, then Turn to page 6 for the Creed

PRAYER OVER THE GIFTS
Lord,
may your apostles join their prayer
   to our offering
and help us to celebrate this sacrifice
   in love and unity.

PREFACE OF SS PETER AND PAUL
The Lord be with you.   **And also with you.**
Lift up your hearts.   **We lift them up to the Lord.**
Let us give thanks to the Lord our God. **It is right to give him thanks and praise.**

Father, all-powerful and ever-living God,
we do well always and everywhere to give you thanks.

You fill our hearts with joy
as we honour your great apostles:
Peter, our leader in the faith,
and Paul, its fearless preacher.

Peter raised up the Church
from the faithful flock of Israel.

Paul brought your call to the nations,
and became the teacher of the world.
Each in his chosen way gathered into unity
the one family of Christ.
Both shared a martyr's death
and are praised throughout the world.

Now, with the apostles and all the angels and saints,
we praise you for ever:

**Holy, holy, holy Lord, God of power and might,
heaven and earth are full of your glory.**
   Hosanna in the highest.
Blessed is he who comes in the name of the Lord.
   Hosanna in the highest.

*Turn to
page 10 for Eucharistic Prayer 1
page 13 for Eucharistic Prayer 2
page 15 for Eucharistic Prayer 3*

COMMUNION ANTIPHON
**Peter said: You are the Christ, the Son of the living God. Jesus answered: You are
Peter, the rock on which I will build my Church.**

PRAYER AFTER COMMUNION
Lord,
renew the life of your Church
with the power of this sacrament.
May the breaking of bread
and the teaching of the apostles
keep us united in your love.

Turn to page 21 for the Concluding Rite

AUGUST 6TH

The Transfiguration of the Lord

As the priest goes to the altar everyone joins in this Entrance Antiphon or a hymn.
**In this shining cloud the Spirit is seen; from it the voice of the Father is heard: This
is my Son, my beloved, in whom is all my delight. Listen to him.**

Turn to page 4

OPENING PRAYER
God our Father,
in the transfigured glory of Christ your Son,
you strengthen our faith
by confirming the witness of your prophets,
and show us the splendour of your beloved sons and daughters.
As we listen to the voice of your Son,
help us to become heirs to eternal life with him
who lives and reigns with you and the Holy Spirit,
one God, for ever and ever.

FIRST READING   A reading from the prophet Daniel
His robe was white as snow.   *Daniel 7:9-10,13-14*

As I watched: Thrones were set in place and one of great age took his seat. His robe
was white as snow, the hair of his head as pure as wool. His throne was a blaze of
flames, its wheels were a burning fire. A stream of fire poured out, issuing from his
presence. A thousand thousand waited on him, ten thousand times ten thousand stood
before him. A court was held and the books were opened. I gazed into the visions of
the night. And I saw, coming on the clouds of heaven, one like a son of man. He came
to the one of great age and was led into his presence. On him was conferred sovereignty,
glory and kingship, and men of all peoples, nations and languages became his servants.
His sovereignty is an eternal sovereignty which shall never pass away, nor will his
empire ever be destroyed.
This is the word of the Lord. **Thanks be to God.**

RESPONSORIAL PSALM   *Psalm 96*
The Lord is king, most high above all the earth.

1. The Lord is king, let earth rejoice,
   let all the coastlands be glad.
   Cloud and darkness are his raiment;
   his throne, justice and right.

2. The mountains melt like wax
   before the Lord of all the earth.
   The skies proclaim his justice;
   all peoples see his glory.

3. For you indeed are the Lord
   most high above all the earth
   exalted far above all spirits.

SECOND READING   A reading from the second letter of St Peter
We heard this ourselves, spoken from heaven.   *2 Peter 1:16-19*

It was not any cleverly invented myths that we were repeating when we brought you
the knowledge of the power and the coming of our Lord Jesus Christ; we had seen his
majesty for ourselves. He was honoured and glorified by God the Father, when the
Sublime Glory itself spoke to him and said, "This is my Son, the Beloved; he enjoys
my favour." We heard this ourselves, spoken from heaven, when we were with him on
the holy mountain.

So we have confirmation of what was said in prophecies; and you will be right to
depend on prophecy and take it as a lamp for lighting a way through the dark until the
dawn comes and the morning star rises in your minds.
This is the word of the Lord. **Thanks be to God.**

All stand to greet the Gospel. If this Acclamation is not sung it may be omitted.
Alleluia, alleluia! This is my Son, the Beloved, he enjoys my favour; listen to him. Alleluia!

GOSPEL   *Matthew 17:1-9*
The Lord be with you. **And also with you.**
A reading from the holy Gospel according to Matthew. **Glory to you, Lord.**

His face shone like the sun.

Jesus took with him Peter and James and his brother John and led them up a high mountain where they could be alone. There in their presence he was transfigured: his face shone like the sun and his clothes became as white as the light. Suddenly Moses and Elijah appeared to them; they were talking with him. Then Peter spoke to Jesus. "Lord," he said "it is wonderful for us to be here; if you wish, I will make three tents here, one for you, one for Moses and one for Elijah." He was still speaking when suddenly a bright cloud covered them with shadow, and from the cloud there came a voice which said, "This is my Son, the Beloved; he enjoys my favour. Listen to him." When they heard this, the disciples fell on their faces, overcome with fear. But Jesus came up and touched them. "Stand up," he said "do not be afraid." And when they raised their eyes they saw no one but only Jesus.
As they came down from the mountain Jesus gave them this order. "Tell no one about the vision until the Son of Man has risen from the dead."
This is the Gospel of the Lord. **Praise to you, Lord Jesus Christ.**

The Homily may follow, then | *Turn to page 6 for the Creed* |

PRAYER OVER THE GIFTS
Lord,
by the transfiguration of your Son
make our gifts holy,
and by his radiant glory free us from
    our sins.

PREFACE OF THE TRANSFIGURATION
The Lord be with you.   **And also with you.**
Lift up your hearts.   **We lift them up to the Lord.**
Let us give thanks to the Lord our God. **It is right to give him thanks and praise.**

Father, all-powerful and ever-living God,
we do well always and everywhere to give you thanks
through Jesus Christ our Lord.

He revealed his glory to the disciples
to strengthen them for the scandal of the cross.
His glory shone from a body like our own,
to show that the Church
which is the body of Christ,
would one day share his glory.

In our unending joy we echo on earth
the song of the angels in heaven
as they praise your glory for ever:

Holy, holy, holy Lord, God of power and might,
heaven and earth are full of your glory.
   Hosanna in the highest.

Blessed is he who comes in the name of the Lord.
   Hosanna in the highest.

Turn to
page 10 for Eucharistic Prayer 1
page 13 for Eucharistic Prayer 2
page 15 for Eucharistic Prayer 3

COMMUNION ANTIPHON
When Christ is revealed we shall be like him, for we shall see him as he is.

PRAYER AFTER COMMUNION
Lord,
you revealed the true radiance of Christ
in the glory of his transfiguration.
May the food we receive from heaven
change us into his image.

Turn to page 21 for the Concluding Rite

AUGUST 15TH

The Assumption

(The Mass for the Vigil is on p.129)

As the priest goes to the altar everyone joins in this Entrance Antiphon or a hymn.

A great sign appeared in heaven: a
woman clothed with the sun, the moon
beneath her feet, and a crown of twelve
stars on her head.

Let us rejoice in the Lord and celebrate
this feast in honour of the Virgin Mary,
at whose assumption the angels rejoice,
giving praise to the Son of God.

Turn to page 4

OPENING PRAYER
All-powerful and ever-living God,
you raised the sinless Virgin Mary,
   mother of your Son,
body and soul to the glory of heaven.
May we see heaven as our final goal
and come to share her glory.

Father in heaven,
all creation rightly gives you praise,
for all life and all holiness come from you.
In the plan of your wisdom
she who bore the Christ in her womb
was raised body and soul in glory to be with
   him in heaven.
May we follow her example in reflecting
your holiness
and join in her hymn of endless life and praise.

FIRST READING   A reading from the book of the Apocalypse

A woman adorned with the sun standing on the moon.   *Apocalypse 11:19;12:1-6,10*

The sanctuary of God in heaven opened, and the ark of the covenant could be seen
inside it. Now a great sign appeared in heaven: a woman, adorned with the sun, standing
on the moon, and with the twelve stars on her head for a crown. She was pregnant,

and in labour, crying aloud in the pangs of childbirth. Then a second sign appeared in the sky, a huge red dragon which had seven heads and ten horns, and each of the seven heads crowned with a coronet. Its tail dragged a third of the stars from the sky and dropped them to the earth, and the dragon stopped in front of the woman as she was having the child, so that he could eat it as soon as it was born from its mother. The woman brought a male child into the world, the son who was to rule all the nations with an iron sceptre, and the child was taken straight up to God and to his throne, while the woman escaped into the desert, where God had made a place of safety ready. Then I heard a voice shout from heaven. "Victory and power and empire for ever have been won by our God, and all authority for his Christ."
This is the word of the Lord. **Thanks be to God.**

RESPONSORIAL PSALM   *Psalm 44*
On your right stands the queen, in garments of gold.

1. The daughters of kings are among
   your loved ones.
   On your right stands the queen in
   gold of Ophir.
   Listen, O daughter, give ear to my words:
   forget your own people and your
   father's house.

2. So will the king desire your beauty:
   he is your lord, pay homage to him.
   They are escorted amid gladness
   and joy;
   pass within the palace of the king.

SECOND READING   A reading from the first letter of St Paul to the Corinthians

Christ as the first-fruits and then those who belong to him.   *1 Corinthians 15:20-26*

Christ has been raised from the dead, the first-fruits of all who have fallen asleep. Death came through one man and in the same way the resurrection of the dead has come through one man. Just as all men die in Adam, so all men will be brought to life in Christ; but all of them in their proper order: Christ as the first-fruits and then, after the coming of Christ, those who belong to him. After that will come the end, when he hands over the kingdom to God the Father, having done away with every sovereignty, authority and power. For he must be king until he has put all his enemies under his feet and the last of the enemies to be destroyed is death, for everything is to be put under his feet.
This is the word of the Lord. **Thanks be to God.**

All stand to greet the Gospel. If this Acclamation is not sung it may be omitted.
Alleluia, alleluia! Mary has been taken up into heaven; all the choirs of angels are rejoicing. Alleluia!

GOSPEL   *Luke 1:39-56*
The Lord be with you. **And also with you.**
A reading from the holy Gospel according to Luke. **Glory to you, Lord.**

The Almighty has done great things for me, he has exalted the lowly.

Mary set out and went as quickly as she could to a town in the hill country of Judah. She went into Zechariah's house and greeted Elizabeth. Now as soon as Elizabeth heard Mary's greeting, the child leapt in her womb and Elizabeth was filled with the Holy Spirit. She gave a loud cry and said, "Of all women you are the most blessed, and blessed is the fruit of your womb. Why should I be honoured with a visit from the mother of my Lord? For the moment your greeting reached my ears, the child in my womb leapt for joy. Yes, blessed is she who believed that the promise made her by the Lord would be fulfilled." And Mary said:

"My soul proclaims the greatness of the Lord and my spirit exults in God my saviour; because he has looked upon his lowly handmaid. Yes, from this day forward all generations will call me blessed, for the Almighty has done great things for me. Holy is his name, and his mercy reaches from age to age for those who fear him. He has shown the power of his arm, he has routed the proud of heart. He has pulled down princes from their thrones and exalted the lowly. The hungry he has filled with good things, the rich sent empty away. He has come to the help of Israel his servant, mindful of his mercy – according to the promise he made to our ancestors – of his mercy to Abraham and to his descendants for ever." Mary stayed with Elizabeth about three months and then went back home.

This is the Gospel of the Lord. **Praise to you, Lord Jesus Christ.**

The Homily follows then   Turn to page 6 for the Creed

PRAYER OVER THE GIFTS
Lord,
receive this offering of our service.
You raised the Virgin Mary to the glory
    of heaven.
By her prayers, help us to seek you
and to live in your love.

PREFACE OF THE ASSUMPTION
The Lord be with you.   **And also with you.**
Lift up your hearts.   **We lift them up to the Lord.**
Let us give thanks to the Lord our God.   **It is right to give him thanks and praise.**

Father, all-powerful and ever-living God,
we do well always and everywhere to give you thanks
through Jesus Christ our Lord.

Today the virgin Mother of God was taken up into heaven
to be the beginning and the pattern of the Church in its perfection
and a sign of hope and comfort for your people on their pilgrim way.
You would not allow decay to touch her body,
for she had given birth to your Son, the Lord of all life,
in the glory of the incarnation.

In our joy we sing to your glory
with all the choirs of angels:

Holy, holy, holy Lord, God of power and might,
heaven and earth are full of your glory.
    Hosanna in the highest.

Blessed is he who comes in the name of the Lord.
    Hosanna in the highest.

Turn to
page 10 for Eucharistic Prayer 1
page 13 for Eucharistic Prayer 2
page 15 for Eucharistic Prayer 3

COMMUNION ANTIPHON
All generations will call me blessed, for the Almighty has done great things for me.

PRAYER AFTER COMMUNION
Lord,
may we who receive this sacrament
   of salvation
be led to the glory of heaven
by the prayers of the Virgin Mary.

Turn to page 21 for the Concluding Rite

NOVEMBER 1ST

All Saints

As the priest goes to the altar everyone joins in this Entrance Antiphon or a hymn.
Let us all rejoice in the Lord and keep a festival in honour of all the saints. Let us join with the angels in joyful praise to the Son of God.

Turn to page 4

OPENING PRAYER
Father, all-powerful and ever-living God,
today we rejoice in the holy men and
   women of every time and place.
May their prayers bring us
   your forgiveness and love.

God our Father,
source of all holiness,
the work of your hands is manifest in
your saints, the beauty of your truth is
   reflected in their faith.
May we who aspire to have part in their
joy be filled with the Spirit that blessed
their lives, so that having shared their
faith on earth we may also know their
peace in your kingdom.

FIRST READING   A reading from the book of the Apocalypse

I saw a huge number, impossible to count, of people from every nation, race, tribe and language.   *Apocalypse 7:2-4, 9-14*

I, John, saw another angel rising where the sun rises, carrying the seal of the living God; he called in a powerful voice to the four angels whose duty was to devastate land and sea, "Wait before you do any damage on land or at sea or to the trees, until we have the seal on the foreheads of the servants of our God." Then I heard how many were sealed: a hundred and forty-four thousand, out of all the tribes of Israel.
After that I saw a huge number, impossible to count, of people from every nation, race, tribe and language; they were standing in front of the throne and in front of the Lamb, dressed in white robes and holding palms in their hands. They shouted aloud, "Victory to our God, who sits on the throne, and to the Lamb!" And all the angels who were standing in a circle round the throne, surrounding the elders and the four animals, prostrated themselves before the throne, and touched the ground with their foreheads, worshipping God with these words, "Amen. Praise and glory and wisdom and thanksgiving and honour and power and strength to our God for ever and ever. Amen." One of the elders then spoke, and asked me. "Do you know who these people are, dressed in white robes, and where they have come from?" I answered him, "You can tell me, my Lord." Then he said, "These are the people who have been through the

great persecution, and they have washed their robes white again in the blood of the Lamb."

This is the word of the Lord. **Thanks be to God.**

RESPONSORIAL PSALM   *Psalm 23*

Such are the men who seek your face, O Lord.

1. The Lord's is the earth and its fullness, the world and all its peoples. It is he who set it on the seas; on the waters he made it firm.

2. Who shall climb the mountain of the Lord? Who shall stand in his holy place? The man with clean hands and pure heart, who desires not worthless things.

3. He shall receive blessings from the Lord and reward from the God who saves him. Such are the men who seek him, seek the face of the God of Jacob.

SECOND READING   A reading from the first letter of St John

We shall see God as he really is.   *1 John 3:1-3*

Think of the love that the Father has lavished on us, by letting us be called God's children; and that is what we are. Because the world refused to acknowledge him, therefore it does not acknowledge us. My dear people, we are already the children of God but what we are to be in the future has not yet been revealed; all we know is, that when it is reavealed we shall be like him because we shall see him as he really is. Surely everyone who entertains this hope must purify himself, must try to be as pure as Christ.

This is the word of the Lord. **Thanks be to God.**

All stand to greet the Gospel. If this Acclamation is not sung it may be omitted.
Alleluia, alleluia! Come to me, all you who labour and are overburdened, and I will give you rest, says the Lord. Alleluia!

GOSPEL   *Matthew 5:1-12*

The Lord be with you. **And also with you.**

A reading from the holy Gospel according to Matthew. **Glory to you, Lord.**

Rejoice and be glad, for your reward will be great in heaven.

Seeing the crowds, Jesus went up the hill. There he sat down and was joined by his disciples. Then he began to speak. This is what he taught them:

"How happy are the poor in spirit; theirs is the kingdom of heaven. Happy the gentle: they shall have the earth for their heritage. Happy those who mourn: they shall be comforted. Happy those who hunger and thirst for what is right: they shall be satisfied. Happy the merciful: they shall have mercy shown them. Happy the pure in heart: they shall see God. Happy the peacemakers: they shall be called sons of God. Happy those who are persecuted in the cause of right: theirs is the kingdom of heaven.

"Happy are you when people abuse you and persecute you and speak all kinds of calumny against you on my account. Rejoice and be glad, for your reward will be great in heaven."

This is the Gospel of the Lord. **Praise to you, Lord Jesus Christ.**

The Homily follows, then | *Turn to page 6 for the Creed*

PRAYER OVER THE GIFTS

Lord,
receive our gifts in honour of the holy
   men and women
who live with you in glory.
May we always be aware
of their concern to help and save us.

PREFACE OF ALL SAINTS

The Lord be with you.   **And also with you.**
Lift up your hearts.   **We lift them up to the Lord.**
Let us give thanks to the Lord our God.   **It is right to give him thanks and praise.**

Father, all-powerful and ever-living God,
we do well always and everywhere to give you thanks.

Today we keep the festival of your holy city,
the heavenly Jerusalem, our mother.
Around your throne
the saints, our brothers and sisters,
sing your praise for ever.
Their glory fills us with joy,
and their communion with us in your Church
gives us inspiration and strength
as we hasten on our pilgrimage of faith,
eager to meet them.

With their great company and all the angels
we praise your glory
as we cry out with one voice:

Holy, holy, holy Lord, God of power and might,
heaven and earth are full of your glory.
   Hosanna in the highest.
Blessed is he who comes in the name of the Lord.
   Hosanna in the highest.

Turn to
page 10 for Eucharistic Prayer 1
page 13 for Eucharistic Prayer 2
page 15 for Eucharistic Prayer 3

COMMUNION ANTIPHON

Happy are the pure of heart for they shall see God. Happy the peacemakers; they shall be called the sons of God. Happy are they who suffer persecution for justice' sake; the kingdom of heaven is theirs.

PRAYER AFTER COMMUNION

Father, holy one,
we praise your glory reflected in the
   saints.
May we who share at this table
be filled with your love
and prepared for the joy of your
   kingdom,
where Jesus is Lord for ever and ever.

Turn to page 21 for
the Concluding Rite

NOVEMBER 2ND
All Souls

(First Mass)
As the priest goes to the altar everyone joins in this Entrance Antiphon or a hymn.
Just as Jesus died and rose again, so will the Father bring with him those who have died in Jesus. Just as in Adam all men die, so in Christ all will be made alive.

| *Turn to page 4* |

OPENING PRAYER
Merciful Father,
hear our prayers and console us.
As we renew our faith in your Son,
whom you raised from the dead,
strengthen our hope that all our
    departed brothers and sisters
will share in his resurrection,
who lives and reigns with you
    and the Holy Spirit,
one God, for ever and ever.

| *In the Liturgy of the Word, other readings may be substituted for those given here.* |

FIRST READING   A reading from the prophet Isaiah
The Lord will destroy death for ever.   *Isaiah 25:6-9*

On this mountain, the Lord of hosts will prepare for all peoples a banquet of rich food. On this mountain, he will remove the mourning veil covering all peoples, and the shroud enwrapping all nations; he will destroy Death for ever. The Lord will wipe away the tears from every cheek; he will take away his people's shame everywhere on earth, for the Lord has said so. That day, it will be said: See, this is God in whom we hoped for salvation; the Lord is the one in whom we hoped. We exult and we rejoice that he has saved us.
This is the word of the Lord. **Thanks be to God.**

ALTERNATIVE FIRST READING   A Reading from the Book of Wisdom
He accepted them as a holocaust.   *Wisdom 3:1-9*

The souls of the virtuous are in the hands of God, no torment shall ever touch them. In the eyes of the unwise, they did appear to die, their going looked like a disaster, their leaving us, like annihilation; but they are in peace. If they experienced punishment as men see it, their hope was rich with immortality; slight was their affliction, great will their blessings be. God has put them to the test and proved them worthy to be with him; he has tested them like gold in a furnace, and accepted them as a holocaust. When the time comes for his visitation they will shine out; as sparks run through the stubble, so will they. They shall judge nations, rule over peoples, and the Lord will be their king for ever. They who trust in him will understand the truth, those who are faithful will live with him in love; for grace and mercy await those he has chosen.
This is the word of the Lord. **Thanks be to God.**

RESPONSORIAL PSALM   *Psalm 22*
The Lord is my shepherd;   *or*   **If I should walk in the valley of darkness**
there is nothing I shall want.   **no evil would I fear,**
                                            for you are there with me.

1. The Lord is my shepherd;   2. He guides me along the right path;
   there is nothing I shall want.   he is true to his name.
   Fresh and green are the pastures   If I should walk in the valley of
   where he gives me repose.   darkness
   Near restful waters he leads me,   no evil would I fear.
   to revive my drooping spirit.   You are there with your crook and
                                                your staff:
                                              with these you give me comfort.

3. You have prepared a banquet for me   4. Surely goodness and kindness shall
   in the sight of my foes.   follow me
   My head you have anointed with oil;   all the days of my life.
   my cup is overflowing.   In the Lord's own house shall I dwell
                                              for ever and ever.

SECOND READING   A reading from the letter of St Paul to the Romans
Having died to make us righteous, is it likely that he would now fail to save us from God's
anger?   *Romans 5:5-11*

Hope is not deceptive, because the love of God has been poured into our hearts by the
Holy Spirit which has been given us. We were still helpless when at his appointed
moment Christ died for sinful men. It is not easy to die even for a good man – though
of course for someone really worthy, a man might be prepared to die – but what proves
that God loves us is that Christ died for us while we were still sinners. Having died to
make us righteous, is it likely that he would now fail to save us from God's anger?
When we were reconciled to God by the death of his Son, we were still enemies; now
that we have been reconciled, surely we may count on being saved by the life of his
Son? Not merely because we have been reconciled but because we are filled with
joyful trust in God, through our Lord Jesus Christ, through whom we have already
gained our reconciliation.
This is the word of the Lord. **Thanks be to God.**

ALTERNATIVE SECOND READING   A reading from the first letter of St Paul
                                                         to the Thessalonians
We shall stay with the Lord for ever.   *1 Thessalonians 4:13-18*

We want you to be quite certain, brothers, about those who have died, to make sure that
you do not grieve about them, like the other people who have no hope. We believe that
Jesus died and rose again, and that it will be the same for those who have died in Jesus:
God will bring them with him. We can tell you this from the Lord's own teaching, that any
of us who are left alive until the Lord's coming will not have any advantage over those
who have died. At the trumpet of God, the voice of the archangel will call out the command
and the Lord himself will come down from heaven; those who have died in Christ will be
the first to rise, and then those of us who are still alive will be taken up in the clouds,
together with them, to meet the Lord in the air. So we shall stay with the Lord for ever.
With such thoughts as these you should comfort one another.
This is the word of the Lord. **Thanks be to God.**

All stand to greet the Gospel. If this Acclamation is not sung it may be omitted.
Alleluia, alleluia! It is my Father's will, says the Lord, that I should lose nothing of all that he has given to me, and that I should raise it up on the last day. Alleluia!

THE GOSPEL   *Matthew 11:25-30*
The Lord be with you. **And also with you.**
A reading from the holy Gospel according to Matthew. **Glory to you, Lord.**
You have hidden these things from the learned and have revealed them to mere children.

Jesus exclaimed: "I bless you, Father, Lord of heaven and of earth, for hiding these things from the learned and the clever and revealing them to mere children. Yes, Father, for that is what it pleased you to do. Everything has been entrusted to me by my Father; and no one except the Son and those to whom the Son chooses to reveal him. "Come to me, all you who labour and are overburdened, and I will give you rest. Shoulder my yoke and learn from me, for I am gentle and humble in heart, and you will find rest for your souls. Yes, my yoke is easy and my burden light."
This is the Gospel of the Lord. **Praise to you, Lord Jesus Christ.**

ALTERNATIVE GOSPEL   *John 11:17-27*
The Lord be with you. **And also with you.**
A reading from the holy Gospel according to Matthew. **Glory to you, Lord.**
I am the resurrection and the life.

On arriving at Bethany, Jesus found that Lazarus had been in the tomb for four days already. Bethany is only about two miles from Jerusalem, and many Jews had come to Martha and Mary to sympathise with them over their brother. When Martha heard that Jesus had come she went to meet him. Mary remained sitting in the house. Martha said to Jesus, "If you had been here, my brother would not have died, but I know that, even now, whatever you ask of God, he will grant you." "Your brother", said Jesus to her, "will rise again." Martha said "I know he will rise again at the resurrection on the last day."
Jesus said:
   "I am the resurrection and the life.
   If anyone believes in me, even though he dies he will live,
   and whoever lives and believes in me
   will never die.
   Do you believe this?"
"Yes, Lord," she said, "I believe that you are the Christ, the Son of God, the one who was to come into this world."
This is the Gospel of the Lord. **Praise to you, Lord Jesus Christ.**

The Homily may follow, then | *Turn to page 7 for the Preparation of the Gifts* |

PRAYER OVER THE GIFTS
Lord,
we are united in this sacrament
by the love of Jesus Christ.
Accept these gifts
and receive our brothers and sisters
into the glory of your Son,
who is Lord for ever and ever.

PREFACE OF CHRISTIAN DEATH 1
An alternative preface of Christian Death may be used.

The Lord be with you.   **And also with you.**
Lift up your hearts.   **We lift them up to the Lord.**
Let us give thanks to the Lord our God.   **It is right to give him thanks and praise.**

Father, all-powerful and ever-living God,
we do well always and everywhere to give you thanks
through Jesus Christ our Lord.

In him, who rose from the dead,
our hope of resurrection dawned.
The sadness of death gives way
to the bright promise of immortality.

Lord, for your faithful people life is changed, not ended.
When the body of our earthly dwelling lies in death
we gain an everlasting dwelling place in heaven.

And so, with all the choirs of angels in heaven
we proclaim your glory
and join in their unending hymn of praise:

Holy, holy, holy Lord, God of power and might,
heaven and earth are full of your glory.
   Hosanna in the highest.
Blessed is he who comes in the name of the Lord.
   Hosanna in the highest.

Turn to
page 10 for Eucharistic Prayer 1
page 13 for Eucharistic Prayer 2
page 15 for Eucharistic Prayer 3

COMMUNION ANTIPHON
I am the resurrection and the life, says the Lord. If anyone believes in me, even
though he dies, he will live. Anyone who lives and believes in me, will not die.

PRAYER AFTER COMMUNION
Lord God,
may the death and resurrection of Christ
which we celebrate in this eucharist
bring the departed faithful to the peace
   of your eternal home.

Turn to page 21 for the
Concluding Rite

NOVEMBER 9TH
Dedication of St John Lateran

As the priest goes to the altar everyone joins in this Entrance Antiphon or a hymn.
I saw the holy city, new Jerusalem, coming down from God out of heaven, like a
bride adorned in readiness for her husband.

Turn to page 4

OPENING PRAYER

God our Father,
from living stones, your chosen people,
you built an eternal temple
   to your glory.
Increase the spiritual gifts you have
   given to your Church,
so that your faithful people may
   continue to grow
into the new and eternal Jerusalem.

Father,
you called your people to be your
Church.
As we gather together in your name,
may we love, honour, and follow you
to eternal life in the kingdom you
promise.

FIRST READING   A reading from the prophet Ezekiel
I saw a stream of water coming from the Temple, bringing life to all wherever it flowed.
Ezekiel 47:1-2,8-9,12

The angel brought me to the entrance of the Temple, where a stream came out from under the Temple threshold and flowed eastwards, since the Temple faced east. The water flowed from under the right side of the Temple, south of the altar. He took me out by the north gate and led me right round outside as far as the outer east gate where the water flowed out on the right-hand side. The man went to the east holding his measuring line and measured off a thousand cubits; he then made me wade across the stream; the water reached my ankles. He measured off another thousand and made me wade across the stream again; the water reached my knees. He measured off another thousand and made me wade across again; the water reached my waist. He measured off another thousand; it was now a river which I could not cross; the stream had swollen and was now deep water, a river impossible to cross. He then said: "Do you see, son of man?" He took me further, then brought me back to the bank of the river. When I got back, there were many trees on each bank of the river. He said, "This water flows east down to the Arabah and to the sea; and flowing into the sea it makes its waters wholesome. Wherever the river flows, all living creatures teeming in it will live. Fish will be very plentiful, for wherever the water goes it brings health, and life teems wherever the river flows. Along the river, on either bank, will grow every kind of fruit tree with leaves that never wither and fruit that never fails; they will bear new fruit every month, because this water comes from the sanctuary. And their fruit will be good to eat and the leaves medicinal."
This is the word of the Lord. **Thanks be to God.**

RESPONSORIAL PSALM   *Psalm 45*
The waters of a river give joy to God's city,
the holy place where the Most High dwells.

1. God is for us a refuge and strength,
   a helper close at hand, in time of
     distress:
   so we shall not fear though the earth
     should rock,
   though the mountains fall into the
     depths of the sea.

2. The waters of a river give joy
    to God's city,
   the holy place where the Most High
    dwells.
   God is within, it cannot be shaken;
   God will help it at the dawning
    of the day.

3. The Lord of hosts is with us:
   the God of Jacob is our stronghold.
   Come, consider the works of the Lord,
   the redoubtable deeds he has done on the earth.

SECOND READING   A reading from St Paul's first letter to the Corinthians
You are the temple of God.   *1 Corinthians 3:9-11,16-17*

You are God's building. By the grace God gave me, I succeeded as an architect and laid the foundations, on which someone else is doing the building. Everyone doing the building must work carefully. For the foundation, nobody can lay any other than the one which has already been laid, that is Jesus Christ.
Didn't you realise that you were God's temple and that the Spirit of God was living among you? If anybody should destroy the temple of God, God will destroy him, because the temple of God is sacred; and you are that temple.
This is the word of the Lord. **Thanks be to God.**

All stand to greet the Gospel. If this Acclamation is not sung, it may be omitted.
Alleluia, alleluia! I have chosen and consecrated this house, says the Lord, for my name to be there for ever. Alleluia!

THE GOSPEL   *John 2:13-22*
The Lord be with you. **And also with you.**
A reading from the holy Gospel according to John. **Glory to you, Lord.**

He was speaking of the sanctuary that was his body.

Just before the Jewish Passover Jesus went up to Jerusalem, and in the Temple he found people selling cattle and sheep and pigeons, and the money-changers sitting at their counters there. Making a whip out of some cord, he drove them all out of the Temple, cattle and sheep as well, scattered the money-changers' coins, knocked their tables over and said to the pigeon-sellers, "Take all this out of here and stop turning my Father's house into a market." Then his disciples remembered the words of scripture: Zeal for your house will devour me. The Jews intervened and said, "What sign can you show us to justify what you have done?" Jesus answered, "Destroy this sanctuary, and in three days I will raise it up." The Jews replied, "It has taken forty-six years to build this sanctuary: are you going to raise it up in three days?" But he was speaking of the sanctuary that was his body, and when Jesus rose from the dead, his disciples remembered that he had said this, and they believed the scripture and the words he had said.
This is the Gospel of the Lord. **Praise to you, Lord Jesus Christ.**

The Homily may follow, then Turn to page 6 for the Creed

PRAYER OVER THE GIFTS
Lord,
receive our gifts.
May we who share this sacrament
experience the life and power it promises,
and hear the answer to our prayers.

PREFACE OF THE DEDICATION OF A CHURCH II
The Lord be with you.   **And also with you.**
Lift up your hearts.   **We lift them up to the Lord.**
Let us give thanks to the Lord our God.   **It is right to give him thanks and praise.**

Father, all-powerful and ever-living God,
we do well always and everywhere to give you thanks.

Your house is a house of prayer,
and your presence makes it a place of blessing.
You give us grace upon grace
to build the temple of your Spirit,
creating its beauty from the holiness of our lives.

Your house of prayer
is also the promise of the Church in heaven.
Here your love is always at work,
preparing the Church on earth
for its heavenly glory
as the sinless bride of Christ,
the joyful mother of a great company of saints.

Now, with the saints and all the angels
we praise you for ever:
Holy, holy, holy Lord, God of power and might,
heaven and earth are full of your glory.
    Hosanna in the highest.
Blessed is he who comes is the name of the Lord.
    Hosanna in the highest.

Turn to
page 10 for Eucharistic Prayer 1
page 13 for Eucharistic Prayer 2
page 15 for Eucharistic Prayer 3

COMMUNION ANTIPHON
Like living stones let yourselves be built on Christ as a spiritual house, a holy
priesthood.

PRAYER AFTER COMMUNION
Father,
you make your Church on earth
a sign of the new and eternal Jerusalem.
By sharing in this sacrament
may we become the temple
    of your presence
the home of your glory.

Turn to page 21 for the Concluding Rite

The Vigil of Pentecost

As the priest goes to the altar everyone joins in this Entrance Antiphon or a hymn.

The love of God has been poured into our hearts by his Spirit living in us, alleluia.

Turn to page 4

OPENING PRAYER
Almighty and ever-living God,
you fulfilled the Easter promise
by sending us your Holy Spirit.
May that Spirit unite the races
   and nations on earth
to proclaim your glory.

or:
God our Father,
you have given us new birth.
Strengthen us with your Holy Spirit
and fill us with your light.

or:
Father in heaven,
fifty days have celebrated the fullness
of the mystery of your revealed love.

See your people gathered in prayer,
open to receive the Spirit's flame.
May it come to rest in our hearts
and disperse the divisions of word
   and tongue.
With one voice and one song
may we praise your name in joy
   and thanksgiving.

FIRST READING: FIRST ALTERNATIVE   A reading from the book of Genesis
It was named Babel because there the language of the whole earth was confused.
Genesis 11:1-9

Throughout the earth men spoke the same language, with the same vocabulary. Now as they moved eastwards they found a plain in the land of Shinar where they settled. They said to one another, "Come, let us make bricks and bake them in the fire." – For stone they used bricks, and for mortar they used bitumen. – "Come," they said "let us build ourselves a town and a tower with its top reaching heaven. Let us make a name for ourselves, so that we may not be scattered about the whole earth."
Now the Lord came down to see the town and the tower that the sons of man had built. "So they are all a single people with a single language!" said the Lord. "This is but the start of their undertakings! There will be nothing too hard for them to do. Come, let us go down and confuse their language on the spot so that they can no longer understand one another." The Lord scattered them thence over the whole face of the earth, and they stopped building the town. It was named Babel therefore, because there the Lord confused the language of the whole earth. It was from there that the Lord scattered them over the whole face of the earth.
This is the word of the Lord. **Thanks be to God.**

FIRST READING: SECOND ALTERNATIVE   A reading from the book of Exodus
The Lord came down on the mountain of Sinai before all the people.
Exodus 19:3-8,16-20

Moses went up to God, and the Lord called to him from the mountain, saying, "Say this to the House of Jacob, declare this to the sons of Israel, 'You yourselves have seen what I did with the Egyptians, how I carried you on eagle's wings and brought you to myself. From this you know that now, if you obey my voice and hold fast to my covenant, you of all the nations shall be my very own, for all the earth is mine. I will count you a kingdom of priests, a consecrated nation.' Those are the words you are to speak to the sons of Israel." So Moses went and summoned the elders of the people, putting before them all that the Lord had bidden him. Then all the people answered as one, "All that the Lord has said, we will do."

Now at daybreak on the third day there were peals of thunder on the mountain and lightning flashes, a dense cloud, and a loud trumpet blast, and inside the camp all the people trembled. Then Moses led the people out of the camp to meet God; and they stood at the bottom of the mountain. The mountain of Sinai was entirely wrapped in smoke, because the Lord had descended on it in the form of fire. Like smoke from a furnace the smoke went up, and the whole mountain shook violently. Louder and louder grew the sound of the trumpet. Moses spoke, and God answered him with peals of thunder. The Lord came down on the mountain of Sinai, on the mountain top, and the Lord called Moses to the top of the mountain.

This is the word of the Lord. **Thanks be to God.**

FIRST READING: THIRD ALTERNATIVE   A reading from the prophet Ezekiel
Dry bones, I am going to make the breath enter you, and you will live.   Ezekiel 37:1-14

The hand of the Lord was laid on me, and he carried me away by the spirit of the Lord and set me down in the middle of a valley, a valley full of bones. He made me walk up and down among them. There were vast quantities of these bones on the ground the whole length of the valley; and they were quite dried up. He said to me, "Son of man, can these bones live?" I said, "You know, Lord." He said, "Prophesy over these bones. Say, 'Dry bones, hear the word of the Lord. The Lord says this to these bones: I am now going to make the breath enter you, and you will live. I shall put sinews on you, I shall make flesh grow on you, I shall cover you with skin and give you breath, and you will live; and you will learn that I am the Lord.' " I prophesied as I had been ordered. While I was prophesying, there was a noise, a sound of clattering; and the bones joined together. I looked, and saw that they were covered with sinews; flesh was growing on them and skin was covering them, but there was no breath in them. He said to me, "Prophesy to the breath; prophesy, son of man. Say to the breath, 'The Lord says this: Come from the four winds, breath; breathe on these dead; let them live!' " I prophesied as he had ordered me, and the breath entered them; they came to life again and stood up on their feet, a great, an immense army.

Then he said, "Son of man, these bones are the whole House of Israel. They keep saying, 'Our bones are dried up, our hope has gone; we are as good as dead.' So prophesy. Say to them, 'The Lord says this: I am now going to open your graves; I mean to raise you from your graves, my people, and lead you back to the soil of Israel. And you will know that I am the Lord, when I open your graves and raise you from your graves, my people. And I shall put my spirit in you, and you will live, and I shall resettle you on your own soil; and you will know that I, the Lord, have said and done this – it is the Lord who speaks.' "

This is the word of the Lord. **Thanks be to God.**

FIRST READING: FOURTH ALTERNATIVE   A reading from the prophet Joel
Even on the slaves, men and women, will I pour out my Spirit.   Joel 3:1-5

Thus says the Lord:
   "I will pour out my spirit on all mankind.
   Your sons and daughters shall prophesy,
   your old men shall dream dreams,
   and your young men see visions.
   Even on the slaves, men and women,

will I pour out my spirit in those days.
I will display portents in heaven and on earth,
blood and fire and columns of smoke."

The sun will be turned into darkness,
and the moon into blood,
before the day of the Lord dawns,
that great and terrible day.
All who call on the name of the Lord will be saved,
for on Mount Zion there will be some who have escaped,
as the Lord has said,
and in Jerusalem some survivors whom the Lord will call.
This is the word of the Lord. **Thanks be to God.**

RESPONSORIAL PSALM
Psalm 103

Send forth your Spirit, O Lord,   *or:* **Alleluia!**
and renew the face of the earth.

1. Bless the Lord, my soul!
   Lord God, how great you are,
   clothed in majesty and glory,
   wrapped in light as in a robe!

2. How many are your works, O Lord!
   In wisdom you have made them all.
   The earth is full of your riches.
   Bless the Lord, my soul.

3. All of these look to you
   to give them their food in due season.
   You give it, they gather it up:
   you open your hand, they have
      their fill.

4. You take back your spirit, they die,
   returning to the dust from which
      they came.
   You send forth your spirit, they are
      created;
   and you renew the face of the earth.

SECOND READING
A reading from the letter of St Paul to the Romans
The Spirit himself expresses our plea in a way that could never be put into words.
Romans 8:22-27

From the beginning till now the entire creation, as we know, has been groaning in one
great act of giving birth; and not only creation, but all of us who possess the first-fruits of
the Spirit, we too groan inwardly as we wait for our bodies to be set free. For we must be
content to hope that we shall be saved – our salvation is not in sight, we should not have
to be hoping for it if it were – but, as I say, we must hope to be saved since we are not
saved yet – it is something we must wait for with patience.
The Spirit too comes to help in our weakness. For when we cannot choose words in order
to pray properly, the Spirit himself expresses our plea in a way that could never be put into
words, and God who knows everything in our hearts knows perfectly well what he means,
and that the pleas of the saints expressed by the Spirit are according to the mind of God.
This is the word of the Lord. **Thanks be to God.**

All stand to greet the Gospel. If this Acclamation is not sung it may be omitted.
**Alleluia, alleluia! Come, Holy Spirit, fill the hearts of your faithful, and kindle in
them the fire of your love. Alleluia!**

THE GOSPEL *John 7:37-39*
The Lord be with you. **And also with you.**
A reading from the holy Gospel according to John. **Glory to you, Lord.**

From his breast shall flow fountains of living water.

On the last day the greatest day of the festival, Jesus stood there and cried out:
"If any man is thirsty, let him come to me!
Let the man come and drink who believes in me!"
As scripture says: From his breast shall flow fountains of living water.
He was speaking of the Spirit which those who believed in him were to receive; for
there was no Spirit as yet because Jesus had not yet been glorified.
This is the Gospel of the Lord. **Praise to you, Lord Jesus Christ.**

The Homily follows, then *Turn to page 6 for the Creed*

PRAYER OVER THE GIFTS
Lord,
send your Spirit on these gifts
and through them help the Church you love
to show your salvation to all the world.

Turn to page 24 for the Preface of Pentecost

COMMUNION ANTIPHON
**On the last day of the festival, Jesus stood and cried aloud: If anyone is thirsty, let
him come to me and drink, alleluia.**
PRAYER AFTER COMMUNION
Lord,
through this eucharist,
send the Holy Spirit of Pentecost into our hearts
to keep us always in your love.

Turn to page 21 for the Concluding Rite

The Vigil of St John the Baptist

As the priest goes to the altar everyone joins in this Entrance Antiphon or a hymn.

**From his mother's womb, he will be filled with the Holy Spirit, he will be great in
the sight of the Lord, and many will rejoice at his birth.**

Turn to page 4

OPENING PRAYER
All-powerful God,
help your people to walk the path to salvation.
By following the teaching of John the Baptist,
may we come to your Son, our Lord Jesus Christ,
who lives and reigns with you and the Holy Spirit,
one God, for ever and ever.

FIRST READING   A reading from the prophet Jeremiah
Before I formed you in the womb, I knew you.   *Jeremiah 1:4-10*

The word of the Lord was addressed to me, saying,
   "Before I formed you in the womb I knew you;
   before you came to birth I consecrated you;
   I have appointed you as prophet to the nations."
I said, "Ah, Lord; look, I do not know how to speak: I am a child!"
   But the Lord replied,
   "Do not say, 'I am a child.'
   Go now to those to whom I send you
   and say whatever I command you.
   Do not be afraid of them,
   for I am with you to protect you –
   it is the Lord who speaks!"
Then the Lord put out his hand and touched my mouth and said to me:
   "There! I am putting my words into your mouth.
   Look, today I am setting you
   over nations and over kingdoms,
   to tear up and to knock down,
   to destroy and to overthrow,
   to build and to plant."
This is the word of the Lord. **Thanks be to God.**

RESPONSORIAL PSALM   *Psalm 70*
From my mother's womb you have been my help.

1. In you, O Lord, I take refuge:
   let me never be put to shame.
   In your justice rescue me, free me:
   pay heed to me and save me.

2. Be a rock where I can take refuge,
   a mighty stronghold to save me;
   for you are my rock, my stronghold.
   Free me from the hand of the wicked.

3. It is you, O Lord, who are my hope,
   my trust, O Lord, since my youth.
   On you I have learned from my birth,
   from my mother's womb you have
      been my help.

4. My lips will tell of your justice
   and day by day of your help.
   O God, you have taught me from
      my youth
   and I proclaim your wonders still.

SECOND READING   A reading from the first letter of St Peter
It was this salvation that the prophets were looking and searching so hard for.

1 Peter 1:8-12

You did not see Jesus Christ, yet you love him; and still without seeing him, you are already filled with a joy so glorious that it cannot be described, because you believe; and you are sure of the end to which your faith looks forward, that is, the salvation of your souls. It was this salvation that the prophets were looking and searching so hard for; their prophecies were about the grace which was to come to you. The Spirit of Christ which was in them foretold the sufferings of Christ and the glories that would come after them, and they tried to find out at what time and in what circumstances all this was to be expected. It was revealed to them that the news they brought of all the things which have now been announced to you, by those who preached to you the Good News through the Holy Spirit sent from heaven, was for you and not for themselves. Even the angels long to catch a glimpse of these things.
This is the word of the Lord. **Thanks be to God.**

All stand to greet the Gospel. If this Acclamation is not sung it may be omitted.
Alleluia, alleluia! He came as a witness, as a witness to speak for the light, preparing for the Lord a people fit for him. Alleluia!

GOSPEL   *Luke 1:5-17*
The Lord be with you. **And also with you.**
A reading from the holy Gospel according to Luke. **Glory to you, Lord.**
She is to bear you a son and you must name him John.

In the days of King Herod of Judaea there lived a priest called Zechariah who belonged to the Abijah section of the priesthood, and he had a wife, Elizabeth by name, who was a descendant of Aaron. Both were worthy in the sight of God, and scrupulously observed all the commandments and observances of the Lord. But they were childless: Elizabeth was barren and they were both getting on in years.
Now it was the turn of Zechariah's section to serve, and he was exercising his priestly office before God when it fell to him by lot, as the ritual custom was, to enter the Lord's sanctuary and burn incense there. And at the hour of incense the whole congregation was outside, praying.
Then there appeared to him the angel of the Lord, standing on the right of the altar of incense. The sight disturbed Zechariah and he was overcome with fear. But the angel said to him, "Zechariah, do not be afraid, your prayer has been heard. Your wife Elizabeth is to bear you a son and you must name him John. He will be your joy and delight and many will rejoice at his birth, for he will be great in the sight of the Lord; he must drink no wine, no strong drink. Even from his mother's womb he will be filled with the Holy Spirit, and he will bring back many of the sons of Israel to the Lord their God. With the spirit and power of Elijah, he will go before him to turn the hearts of fathers towards their children and the disobedient back to the wisdom that the virtuous have, preparing for the Lord a people fit for him."
This is the Gospel of the Lord. **Praise to you, Lord Jesus Christ.**

The Homily follows, then Turn to page 6 for the Creed

PRAYER OVER THE GIFTS
Lord,
look with favour on the gifts we bring
on this feast of John the Baptist.
Help us put into action
the mystery we celebrate in this sacrament.

Turn to page 100 for the Preface of St John the Baptist

COMMUNION ANTIPHON
Blessed be the Lord God of Israel, for he has visited and redeemed his people.

PRAYER AFTER COMMUNION
Father,
may the prayers of John the Baptist
lead us to the Lamb of God.
May this eucharist bring us the mercy of Christ,
who is Lord for ever and ever.

Turn to page 21 for the Concluding Rite

The Vigil of Ss Peter and Paul

As the priest goes to the altar everyone joins in this Entrance Antiphon or a hymn.
Peter the apostle and Paul the teacher of the Gentiles have brought us to know the law of the Lord.

Turn to page 4

OPENING PRAYER
Lord our God,
encourage us through the prayers
    of Saints Peter and Paul.
May the apostles who strengthened
    the faith of the infant Church
help us on our way of salvation.

or: Father in heaven,
the light of your revelation brought
    Peter and Paul
the gift of faith in Jesus your Son.

Through their prayers
may we always give thanks for your life
given us in Christ Jesus,
and for having been enriched by him
in all knowledge and love.

FIRST READING   A reading from the Acts of the Apostles

I will give you what I have: in the name of Jesus stand up and walk!   *Acts 3:1-10*

Once, when Peter and John were going up to the Temple for the prayers at the ninth hour, it happened that there was a man being carried past. He was a cripple from birth; and they used to put him down every day near the Temple entrance called the Beautiful Gate so that he could beg from the people going in. When this man saw Peter and John on their way into the Temple he begged from them. Both Peter and John looked straight at him and said, "Look at us." He turned to them expectantly, hoping to get something from them, but Peter said, "I have neither silver nor gold, but I will give you what I have: in the name of Jesus Christ the Nazarene, walk!" Peter then took him by the hand and helped him to stand up. Instantly his feet and ankles became firm, he jumped up, stood, and began to walk, and he went with them into the Temple, walking and jumping and praising God. Everyone could see him walking and praising God, and they recognised him as the man who used to sit begging at the Beautiful Gate of the Temple. They were all astonished and unable to explain what had happened to him.

This is the word of the Lord. **Thanks be to God.**

RESPONSORIAL PSALM   *Psalm 18*
Their word goes forth through all the earth.

1. The heavens proclaim the glory of God
   and the firmament shows forth the work of his hands.
   Day unto day takes up the story
   and night unto night makes known the message.

2. No speech, no word, no voice is heard
   yet their span extends through all the earth,
   their words to the utmost bounds of the world.

SECOND READING   A reading from the letter of St Paul to the Galatians

God specially chose me while I was still in my mother's womb.   *Galatians 1:11-20*

The Good News I preached is not a human message that I was given by men, it is something I learnt only through a revelation of Jesus Christ. You must have heard of my career as a practising Jew, how merciless I was in persecuting the Church of God, how much damage I did to it, how I stood out among other Jews of my generation, and how enthusiastic I was for the traditions of my ancestors.

Then God, who had specially chosen me while I was still in my mother's womb, called me through his grace and chose to reveal his Son to me, so that I might preach the Good News about him to the pagans. I did not stop to discuss this with any human being, nor did I go up to Jerusalem to see those who were already apostles before me, but I went off to Arabia at once and later went straight back from there to Damascus. Even when after three years I went up to Jerusalem to visit Cephas and stayed with him for fifteen days, I did not see any of the other apostles; I only saw James, the brother of the Lord, and I swear before God that what I have just written is the literal truth.

This is the word of the Lord. **Thanks be to God.**

All stand to greet the Gospel. If this Acclamation is not sung it may be omitted.
Alleluia, alleluia! Lord, you know everything; you know I love you. Alleluia!

GOSPEL *John 21:15-19*
The Lord be with you. **And also with you.**
A reading from the holy Gospel according to John. **Glory to you, Lord.**

Feed my lambs, feed my sheep.

Jesus showed himself to his disciples, and after they had eaten he said to Simon Peter, "Simon son of John, do you love me more than these others do?" He answered, "Yes Lord, you know I love you." Jesus said to him, "Feed my lambs." A second time he said to him, "Simon son of John, do you love me?" He replied, "Yes, Lord, you know I love you." Jesus said to him, "Look after my sheep." Then he said to him a third time, "Simon son of John, do you love me?" Peter was upset that he asked him the third time, "Do you love me?" and said, "Lord, you know everything; you know I love you." Jesus said to him, "Feed my sheep.

> "I tell you most solemnly,
> when you were young
> you put on your own belt
> and walked where you liked;
> but when you grow old
> you will stretch out your hands,
> and somebody else will put a belt round you
> and take you where you would rather not go."

In these words he indicated the kind of death by which Peter would give glory to God. After this he said, "Follow me."
This is the Gospel of the Lord. **Praise to you, Lord Jesus Christ.**

The Homily follows, then Turn to page 6 for the Creed

PRAYER OVER THE GIFTS
Lord,
we present these gifts
on this feast of the apostles Peter and Paul.
Help us to know our own weakness
and to rejoice in your saving power.

Turn to page 103 for the Preface of Ss Peter and Paul

COMMUNION ANTIPHON
Simon, son of John, do you love me more than these? Lord, you know all things; you know that I love you.

PRAYER AFTER COMMUNION
Father,
you give us light by the teaching of your apostles.
In this sacrament we have received
fill us with your strength.

Turn to page 21 for the Concluding Rite

The Vigil of the Assumption

As the priest goes to the altar everyone joins in this Entrance Antiphon or a hymn.
All honour to you, Mary! Today you were raised above the choirs of angels to lasting glory with Christ.

Turn to page 4

OPENING PRAYER

Almighty God,
you gave a humble virgin
the privilege of being the mother
  of your Son,
and crowned her with the glory
  of heaven.
May the prayers of the Virgin Mary
bring us to the salvation of Christ
and raise us up to eternal life.

or:

Almighty Father of our Lord Jesus Christ,
you have revealed the beauty
  of your power
by exalting the lowly virgin of Nazareth
and making her the mother of our Saviour.
May the prayers of this woman clothed
  with the sun
bring Jesus to the waiting world
and fill the void of incompletion
with the presence of her child,
who lives and reigns with you and
  the Holy Spirit,
one God, for ever and ever.

FIRST READING   A reading from the first book of Chronicles
They brought in the ark of God and set it inside the tent which David had pitched for it.

1 Chronicles 15:3-4,15-16;16:1-2

David gathered all Israel together in Jerusalem to bring the ark of God up to the place he had prepared for it. David called together the sons of Aaron and the sons of Levi. And the Levites carried the ark of God with the shafts on their shoulders, as Moses had ordered in accordance with the word of the Lord. David then told the heads of the Levites to assign duties for their kinsmen as cantors, with their various instruments of music, harps and lyres and cymbals, to play joyful tunes. They brought the ark of God in and put it inside the tent that David had pitched for it; and they offered holocausts before God, and communion sacrifices. And when David had finished offering holocausts and communion sacrifices, he blessed the people in the name of the Lord.
This is the word of the Lord. **Thanks be to God.**

RESPONSORIAL PSALM   *Psalm 131*
**Go up, Lord, to the place of your rest,
you and the ark of your strength.**

1. At Ephrata we heard of the ark;
   we found it in the plains of Yearim.
   "Let us go to the place
     of his dwelling;
   let us go to kneel at his footstool."

2. Your priests shall be clothed
     with holiness:
   your faithful shall ring out their joy.
   For the sake of David your servant
   do not reject your anointed.

3. For the Lord has chosen Zion;
   he has desired it for his dwelling:
   "This is my resting-place for ever,
   here have I chosen to live."

SECOND READING   A reading from the first letter of St Paul to the Corinthians
He gave us victory through our Lord Jesus Christ.   *1 Corinthians 15:54-57*

When this perishable nature has put on imperishability, and when this mortal nature has put on immortality, then the words of scripture will come true: Death is swallowed up in victory. Death, where is your victory? Death, where is your sting? Now the sting of death is sin and sin gets its power from the Law. So let us thank God for giving us the victory through our Lord Jesus Christ.
This is the word of the Lord. **Thanks be to God.**

All stand to greet the Gospel. If this Acclamation is not sung it may be omitted.
Alleluia, alleluia! Happy are those who hear the word of God, and keep it. Alleluia!

GOSPEL   *Luke 11:27-28*
The Lord be with you. **And also with you.**
A reading from the holy Gospel according to Luke. **Glory to you, Lord.**

As Jesus was speaking, a woman in the crowd raised her voice and said, "Happy the womb that bore you and the breasts you sucked!" But he replied, "Still happier those who hear the word of God and keep it!"
This is the Gospel of the Lord. **Praise to you, Lord Jesus Christ.**

The Homily follows, then   Turn to page 6 for the Creed

PRAYER OVER THE GIFTS
Lord,
receive this sacrifice of praise and peace
in honour of the assumption of the Mother of God.
May our offering bring us pardon
and make our lives a thanksgiving to you.

Turn to page 109 for the Preface of the Assumption

COMMUNION ANTIPHON
Blessed is the womb of the Virgin Mary; she carried the Son of the eternal Father.

PRAYER AFTER COMMUNION
God of mercy,
we rejoice because Mary, the mother of our Lord,
was taken into the glory of heaven.
May the holy food we receive at this table
free us from evil.

Turn to page 21 for the Concluding Rite

Eucharistic Prayer for Children I

The Lord be with you.
And also with you.

Lift up your hearts.
We lift them up to the Lord.

Let us give thanks to the Lord our God.
It is right to give him thanks and praise.

God our Father,
you have brought us here together
so that we can give you thanks and praise
for all the wonderful things you have done.

We thank you for all that is beautiful in the world
and for the happiness you have given us.
We praise you for daylight
and for your word which lights up our minds.
We praise you for the earth,
and all the people who live on it,
and for our life which comes from you.

We know that you are good.
You love us and do great things for us.
[So we all sing (say) together:
Holy, holy, holy Lord, God of power and might,
heaven and earth are full of your glory.
    Hosanna in the highest.]

Father,
you are always thinking about your people;
you never forget us.
You sent us your Son Jesus,
who gave his life for us
and who came to save us.
He cured sick people;
he cared for those who were poor
and wept with those who were sad.
He forgave sinners
and taught us to forgive each other.
He loved everyone
and showed us how to be kind.
He took children in his arms and blessed them.
[So we are glad to sing (say):
Blessed is he who comes in the name of the Lord.
    Hosanna in the highest.]

God our Father,
all over the world your people praise you.
So now we pray with the whole Church:
with *N.*, our pope and *N.*, our bishop.
In heaven the blessed Virgin Mary,
the apostles and all the saints
always sing your praise.
Now we join with them and with the angels
to adore you as we sing (say):
Holy, holy, holy Lord, God of power and might,
heaven and earth are full of your glory.
    Hosanna in the highest.

Blessed is he who comes in the name of the Lord.
    Hosanna in the highest.

God our Father,
you are most holy
and we want to show you that we are grateful.

We bring you bread and wine
and ask you to send your Holy Spirit to make
    these gifts
the body + and blood of Jesus your Son.
Then we can offer to you
what you have given to us.

On the night before he died,
Jesus was having supper with his apostles.
He took bread from the table.
He gave you thanks and praise.
Then he broke the bread, gave it to his friends,
    and said:

Take this, all of you, and eat it:
this is my body which will be given up for you.

When supper was ended,
Jesus took the cup that was filled with wine.
He thanked you, gave it to his friends, and said:

Take this, all of you, and drink from it:
this is the cup of my blood,
the blood of the new and everlasting covenant.
It will be shed for you and for all
so that sins may be forgiven.
Do this in memory of me.

We do now what Jesus told us to do.
We remember his death and his resurrection
and we offer you, Father, the bread that
    gives us life,
and the cup that saves us.
Jesus brings us to you;
welcome us as you welcome him.

Let us proclaim our faith:
All say: **1   Christ has died,**
                Christ is risen,
                Christ will come again.

2   Dying you destroyed our death,
    rising you restored our life.
    Lord Jesus, come in glory.

3   When we eat this bread and drink this cup,
    we proclaim your death, Lord Jesus,
    until you come in glory.

4   Lord, by your cross and resurrection
    you have set us free.
    You are the Saviour of the world.

Father,
because you love us,
you invite us to come to your table.
Fill us with the joy of the Holy Spirit
as we receive the body and blood of your Son.

Lord,
you never forget any of your children.
We ask you to take care of those we love,
especially of *N.* and *N.*,
and we pray for those who have died.

Remember everyone who is suffering from pain
or sorrow.
Remember Christians everywhere
and all other people in the world.

We are filled with wonder and praise
when we see what you do for us
through Jesus your Son,
and so we sing (say):

Through him,
with him,
in him,
in the unity of the Holy Spirit,
all glory and honour is yours,
almighty Father,
for ever and ever.
Amen.

Turn to page 21 for the Communion Rite

Eucharistic Prayer for Children II

The Lord be with you.
And also with you.

Lift up your hearts.
We lift them up to the Lord.

Let us give thanks to the Lord our God.
It is right to give him thanks and praise.

God, our loving Father,
we are glad to give you thanks and praise
because you love us.
With Jesus we sing your praise:

All say:
Glory to God in the highest.

or:
Hosanna in the highest.

Because you love us,
you gave us this great and beautiful world.
With Jesus we sing your praise:

Glory to God in the highest.

or:
Hosanna in the highest.

Because you love us,
you sent Jesus your Son
to bring us to you
and to gather us around him
as the children of one family.
With Jesus we sing your praise:

Glory to God in the highest.

or:
Hosanna in the highest.

For such great love
we thank you with the angels and saints
as they praise you and sing (say):

**Holy, holy, holy Lord, God of power and might,
heaven and earth are full of your glory.
Hosanna in the highest.**

**Blessed is he who comes in the name of the Lord.
Hosanna in the highest.**

Blessed be Jesus, whom you sent
to be the friend of children and of the poor.

He came to show us
how we can love you, Father,
by loving one another.
He came to take away sin,
which keeps us from being friends,
and hate, which makes us all unhappy.

He promised to send the Holy Spirit,
to be with us always
so that we can live as your children.

All say:
**Blessed is he who comes in the name of the Lord.
Hosanna in the highest.**

God our Father,
we now ask you
to send your Holy Spirit
to change these gifts of bread and wine
into the body + and blood
of Jesus Christ, our Lord.

The night before he died,
Jesus your Son showed us how much you love us.
When he was at supper with his disciples,

he took bread,
and gave you thanks and praise.
Then he broke the bread,
gave it to his friends, and said:

Take this, all of you, and eat it:
this is my body which will be given up for you.

He shows the consecrated host to the people while all say:
Jesus has given his life for us.

When supper was ended,
Jesus took the cup that was filled with wine.
He thanked you, gave it to his friends, and said:

Take this, all of you, and drink from it:
this is the cup of my blood,
the blood of the new and everlasting covenant.
It will be shed for you and for all
so that sins may be forgiven.

He shows the chalice to the people while all say:
Jesus has given his life for us.

The priest continues:

Then he said to them:
Do this in memory of me.

And so, loving Father,
we remember that Jesus died and rose again
to save the world.
He put himself into our hands
to be the sacrifice we offer you.

All say:
We praise you, we bless you, we thank you.

Lord our God,
listen to our prayer.

Send the Holy Spirit
to all of us who share in this meal.
May this Spirit bring us closer together
in the family of the Church,
with *N.*, our pope,
N., our bishop,
all other bishops,
and all who serve your people.

We praise you, we bless you, we thank you.

Remember, Father, our families and friends *N.*,
and all those we do not love as we should.
Remember those who have died *N.*
Bring them home to you
to be with you for ever.

We praise you, we bless you, we thank you.

Gather us all together into your kingdom.
There we shall be happy for ever
with the Virgin Mary, Mother of God and
    our mother.

There all the friends
of Jesus the Lord
will sing a song of joy.

We praise you, we bless you, we thank you.

Through him,
with him,
in him,
in the unity of the Holy Spirit,
all glory and honour is yours,
almighty Father,
for ever and ever.
Amen.

Turn to page 21 for the Communion Rite

Eucharistic Prayer for Children III

The Lord be with you.
And also with you.

Lift up your hearts.
We lift them up to the Lord.

Let us give thanks to the Lord our God.
It is right to give him thanks and praise.

Outside the Easter Season

We thank you,
God our Father.

You made us to live for you and for each other.
We can see and speak to one another,

and become friends,
and share our joys and sorrows.

And so, Father, we gladly thank you
with every one who believes in you;
with the saints and the angels,
we rejoice and praise you, saying:

**Holy, holy, holy Lord, God of power
    and might,
heaven and earth are full of your glory.
    Hosanna in the highest.**

**Blessed is he who comes in the name of
    the Lord.
    Hosanna in the highest.**

Yes, Lord, you are holy;
you are kind to us and to all men.
For this we thank you.
We thank you above all for your Son, Jesus Christ.

You sent him into this world
because people had turned away from you
and no longer loved each other.
He opened our eyes and our hearts
to understand that we are brothers and sisters
and that you are Father of us all.

He now brings us together to one table
and asks us to do what he did.

During the Easter Season

We thank you,
God our Father.

You are the living God;
you have called us to share in your life,
and to be happy with you for ever.
You raised up Jesus, your Son,
the first among us to rise from the dead,
and gave him new life.
You have promised to give us new life also,
a life that will never end,
a life with no more anxiety and suffering.

And so, Father, we gladly thank you
with every one who believes in you;
with the saints and the angels,
we rejoice and praise you, saying:

Holy, holy, holy Lord ...

Yes, Lord, you are holy;
you are kind to us and to all men.
For this we thank you.
We thank you above all for your Son, Jesus Christ.

He brought us the good news
of life to be lived with you for ever in heaven.
He showed us the way to that life,
the way of love.
He himself has gone that way before us.

He now brings us together to one table
and asks us to do what he did.

Father,
we ask you to bless these gifts of bread and wine
and make them holy.

Change them for us into the body + and blood
of Jesus Christ, your Son.
On the night before he died for us,
he had supper for the last time with his disciples.

He took bread
and gave you thanks.

He broke the bread
and gave it to his friends, saying:

Take this, all of you, and eat it:
this is my body which will be given up for you.

In the same way he took a cup of wine.
He gave you thanks
and handed the cup to his disciples, saying:

Take this, all of you, and drink from it:
this is the cup of my blood,
the blood of the new and everlasting covenant.
It will be shed for you and for all
so that sins may be forgiven.
Do this in memory of me.

God our Father,
we remember with joy
all that Jesus did to save us.
In this holy sacrifice,
which he gave as a gift to his Church,
we remember his death and resurrection.

Father in heaven,
accept us together with your beloved Son.
He willingly died for us,
but you raised him to life again.
We thank you and say:

Glory to God in the highest (or some other
    suitable acclamation of praise).

Jesus now lives with you in glory,
but he is also here on earth, among us.
We thank you and say:

Glory to God in the highest.

One day he will come in glory
and in his kingdom
there will be no more suffering,
no more tears, no more sadness.
We thank you and say:

Glory to God in the highest.

Father in heaven,
you have called us
to receive the body and blood of Christ
    at this table
and to be filled with the joy of the Holy Spirit.
Through this sacred meal
give us strength to please you more and more.

Lord, our God,
remember *N.*, our pope,
N., our bishop, and all other bishops.

Outside the Easter Season

Help all who follow Jesus
to work for peace
and to bring happiness to others.

During the Easter Season

Fill all Christians with the gladness of Easter.
Help us to bring this joy
to all who are sorrowful.

Bring us all at last
together with Mary, the Mother of God,
and all the saints,
to live with you
and to be one with Christ in heaven.

Through him,
with him,
in him,
in the unity of the Holy Spirit
all glory and honour is yours,
almighty Father,
for ever and ever.

Amen.

Turn to page 21 for the Communion Rite.

Eucharistic Prayer for Reconciliation I

The Lord be with you.
And also with you.

Lift up your hearts.
We lift them up to the Lord.

Let us give thanks to the Lord our God.
It is right to give him thanks and praise.

Father, all-powerful and ever-living God,
we do well always and everywhere to give you
thanks and praise.

You never cease to call us
to a new and more abundant life.

God of love and mercy,
you are always ready to forgive;
we are sinners,
and you invite us
to trust in your mercy.

Time and time again
we broke your covenant,
but you did not abandon us.
Instead, through your Son, Jesus our Lord,
you bound yourself even more closely
to the human family
by a bond that can never be broken.

Now is the time
for your people to turn back to you
and to be renewed in Christ your Son,
a time of grace and reconciliation.

You invite us
to serve the family of mankind
by opening our hearts
to the fullness of your Holy Spirit.

In wonder and gratitude,
we join our voices with the choirs of heaven
to proclaim the power of your love
and to sing of our salvation in Christ:

Holy, holy, holy Lord, God of power and might,
heaven and earth are full of your glory.
Hosanna in the highest.

Blessed is he who comes in the name of the Lord.
Hosanna in the highest.

Father,
from the beginning of time
you have always done what is good for man
so that we may be holy as you are holy.

Look with kindness on your people
gathered here before you:
send forth the power of your Spirit
so that these gifts may become for us
the body + and blood of your beloved Son,
Jesus the Christ,
in whom we have become your sons
and daughters.

When we were lost
and could not find the way to you,
you loved us more than ever:
Jesus, your Son, innocent and without sin,
gave himself into our hands
and was nailed to a cross.
Yet before he stretched out his arms between
heaven and earth
in the everlasting sign of your covenant,
he desired to celebrate the Paschal feast
in the company of his disciples.

While they were at supper,
he took bread and gave you thanks and praise.
He broke the bread, gave it to his disciples,
and said:

Take this, all of you, and eat it:
this is my body which will be given up for you.

At the end of the meal,
knowing that he was to reconcile all things
in himself
by the blood of his cross,
he took the cup, filled with wine.
Again he gave you thanks, handed the cup to his
friends, and said:

Take this, all of you, and drink from it:
this is the cup of my blood,
the blood of the new and everlasting covenant.
It will be shed for you and for all
so that sins may be forgiven.
Do this in memory of me.

Let us proclaim the mystery of faith:

1 **Christ has died,**
   Christ is risen,
   Christ will come again.

2 **Dying you destroyed our death,**
   rising you restored our life.
   Lord Jesus, come in glory.

3 **When we eat this bread and drink this cup,**
   we proclaim your death, Lord Jesus,
   until you come in glory.

4 **Lord, by your cross and resurrection**
   you have set us free.
   You are the Saviour of the world.

We do this in memory of Jesus Christ,
our Passover and our lasting peace.
We celebrate his death and resurrection
and look for the coming of that day
when he will return to give us the fullness
   of joy.
Therefore we offer you, God ever faithful
   and true,
the sacrifice which restores men to your
   friendship.

Father,
look with love
on those you have called
to share in the one sacrifice of Christ.
By the power of your Holy Spirit
make them one body,
healed of all division.

Keep us all
in communion of mind and heart
with *N.*, our pope, and *N.*, our bishop
   [and his assistant bishops].
Help us to work together
for the coming of your kingdom,
until at last we stand in your presence
to share the life of the saints,
in the company of the virgin Mary
   and the apostles,
and of our departed brothers and sisters
whom we commend to your mercy.

Then, freed from every shadow of death,
we shall take our place in the new creation
and give you thanks
with Christ, our risen Lord.

Through him,
with him,
in him,
in the unity of the Holy Spirit,
all glory and honour is yours,
almighty Father,
for ever and ever.

Amen.

Turn to page 21 for the Communion Rite

Eucharistic Prayer for Reconciliation II

The Lord be with you.
And also with you.

Lift up your hearts.
We lift them up to the Lord.

Let us give thanks to the Lord our God.
It is right to give him thanks and praise.

Father, all-powerful and ever-living God,
we praise and thank you through Jesus Christ
   our Lord
for your presence and action in the world.

In the midst of conflict and division,
we know it is you
who turn our minds to thoughts of peace.
Your Spirit changes our hearts:
enemies begin to speak to one another,

those who were estranged join hands
   in friendship,
and nations seek the way of peace together.

Your Spirit is at work
when understanding puts an end to strife,
when hatred is quenched by mercy,
and vengeance gives way to forgiveness.

For this we should never cease
to thank and praise you.
We join with all the choirs of heaven
as they sing for ever to your glory:

Holy, holy, holy Lord, God of power and might,
heaven and earth are full of your glory.
   Hosanna in the highest.
Blessed is he who comes in the name of the Lord.
   Hosanna in the highest.

God of power and might,
we praise you through your Son, Jesus Christ,
who comes in your name.
He is the word that brings salvation.
He is the hand you stretch out to sinners.
He is the way that leads to your peace.

God our Father,
we had wandered far from you,
but through your Son you have brought us back.
You gave him up to death
so that we might turn again to you
and find our way to one another.

Therefore we celebrate the reconciliation
Christ has gained for us.

We ask you to sanctify these gifts
by the power of your Spirit,
as we now fulfill your Son's + command.

While he was at supper
on the night before he died for us,
he took bread in his hands,
and gave you thanks and praise.
He broke the bread,
gave it to his disciples, and said:

Take this, all of you, and eat it:
this is my body which will be given up for you.

At the end of the meal he took the cup.
Again he praised you for your goodness,
gave the cup to his disciples, and said:

Take this, all of you, and drink from it:
this is the cup of my blood,
the blood of the new and everlasting covenant.
It will be shed for you and for all
so that sins may be forgiven.
Do this in memory of me.

Let us proclaim the mystery of faith:

1. **Christ has died,**
   Christ is risen,
   Christ will come again.

2. **Dying you destroyed our death,**
   rising you restored our life.
   Lord Jesus, come in glory.

3. **When we eat this bread and drink this cup,**
   we proclaim your death, Lord Jesus,
   until you come in glory.

4. **Lord, by your cross and resurrection**
   you have set us free.
   You are the Saviour of the world.

Lord our God,
your Son has entrusted to us
this pledge of his love.
We celebrate the memory of his death
   and resurrection
and bring you the gift you have given us,
the sacrifice of reconciliation.
Therefore, we ask you, Father,
to accept us, together with your Son.

Fill us with his Spirit
through our sharing in this meal.
May he take away all that divides us.

May this Spirit keep us always in communion
with *N.*, our pope, *N.*, our bishop
   [and his assistant bishops],
all the bishops and all your people.
Father, make your Church throughout the world
a sign of unity and an instrument of your peace.

You have gathered us here
around the table of your Son,
in fellowship with the virgin Mary,
   Mother of God,
and all the saints.

In that new world where the fullness of your
   peace will be revealed,
gather people of every race, language, and way
   of life
to share in the one eternal banquet
with Jesus Christ the Lord.

Through him,
with him,
in him,
in the unity of the Holy Spirit,
all glory and honour is yours,
almighty Father,
for ever and ever.

Amen.

Turn to page 21 for the Communion Rite.

Eucharistic Prayer
for Masses for Various Needs and Occasions

The Lord be with you.
And also with you.

Lift up your hearts.
We lift them up to the Lord.

Let us give thanks to the Lord our God.
It is right to give him thanks and praise.

A. *The Church on the Way to Unity*

It is truly right to give you thanks,
it is fitting that we sing of your glory,
Father of infinite goodness.

Through the gospel proclaimed by your Son
you have brought together in a single Church
people of every nation, culture, and tongue.
Into it you breathe the power of your Spirit,
that in every age
your children may be gathered as one.

Your Church bears steadfast witness to your love.
It nourishes our hope for the coming of your kingdom
and is a sure sign of the lasting covenant
which you promised us in Jesus Christ our Lord.

Therefore heaven and earth sing forth your praise
while we, with all the Church,
proclaim your glory without end:

B. *God Guides the Church on the Way of Salvation*

It is truly right and just,
our duty and our salvation
always and everywhere to give you thanks,
Lord, holy Father,
creator of the world and source of all life.

You never abandon the creatures formed by your wisdom,
but remain with us and work for our good even now.
With mighty hand and outstretched arm
you led your people, Israel, through the desert.
By the power of the Holy Spirit
you guide your pilgrim Church today
as it journeys along the paths of time
to the eternal joy of your kingdom,
through Christ our Lord.
Now, with all the angels and saints
we praise your glory without end:

C. Jesus, Way to the Father

It is truly right and just,
our duty and our salvation
always and everywhere to give you thanks,
Father of holiness, Lord of heaven and earth.

Through your eternal Word you created all things
and govern their course with infinite wisdom.
In the Word made flesh
you have given us a mediator
who has spoken your words to us
and called us to follow him.
He is the way that leads to you,
the truth that sets us free,
the life that makes our joy complete.

Through your Son
you gather into one family, men and women
created for the glory of your name,
redeemed by the blood of the cross,
and sealed with the Holy Spirit.

And so we praise your mighty deeds
and join with the hosts of angels,
as they proclaim your glory without end:

D. Jesus, the Compassion of God

It is truly right to give you thanks,
it is fitting that we offer you praise,
Father of mercy, faithful God.

You sent Jesus Christ your Son among us
as redeemer and Lord.
He was moved with compassion
for the poor and the powerless,
for the sick and the sinner;
he made himself neighbour to the oppressed.
By his rods and actions
he proclaimed to the world
that you care for us
as a father cares for his children.

And so, with all the angels and saints
we sing the joyful hymn of your praise:

Holy, holy, holy Lord God of power and might,
heaven and earth are full of your glory.
Hosanna in the highest.
Blessed is he who comes in the name of the Lord.
Hosanna in the highest.

Blessed are you, God of holiness:
you accompany us with love
as we journey through life.

Blessed too is your Son, Jesus Christ,
who is present among us
and whose love gathers us together.
As once he did for his disciples,
Christ now opens the scriptures for us and breaks the bread.

Great and merciful Father, we ask you:
send down your Holy Spirit
to hallow these gifts of bread and wine,
that they may become for us

the body + and blood of our Lord, Jesus Christ.

On the eve of his passion and death,
while at the table with those he love,
he took bread and gave you thanks;
he broke the bread,
gave it to his disciples, and said:

Take this, all of you, and eat it:
this is my body which will be given up for you.

When supper was ended, he took the cup;
again, he gave you thanks
and, handing the cup to his disciples, he said:

Take this, all of you, and drink from it:
this is the cup of my blood,
the blood of the new and everlasting covenant.
It will be shed for you and for all
so that sins may be forgiven.

Do this in memory of me.

Let us proclaim the mystery of faith:

A. **Christ has died,
Christ is risen,
Christ will come again.**

B. **Dying you destroyed our death,
rising you restored our life.
Lord Jesus, come in glory.**

C. **When we eat this bread and drink this cup,
we proclaim your death, Lord Jesus,
until you come in glory.**

D. **Lord, by your cross and resurrection
you have set us free.
You are the Saviour of the world.**

And so, Father most holy,
we celebrate the memory of Christ, your Son,
whom you led through suffering and death on the cross
to the glory of the resurrection
and a place at your right hand.

Until Jesus, our Saviour, comes again,
we proclaim the work of your love,
and we offer you the bread of life
and the cup of eternal blessing.

Look with favour on the offering of your Church
in which we show forth the paschal sacrifice of Christ entrusted to us.
Through the power of your Spirit of love
include us now and for ever
among the members of your Son,
whose body and blood we share.

A. The Church on the Way to Unity

Renew by the light of the gospel
the Church of N. [diocese/place].
Strengthen the bonds of unity between the faithful and their pastors,
that together with N. our pope, N. our bishop,
and the whole college of bishops,
your people may stand forth
in a world torn by conflict and strife
as a sign of oneness and peace.

B. God Guides the Church on the Way of Salvation

Strengthen in unity
those you have called to this table.
Together with N. our pope, N. our bishop,
with all bishops, priests, and deacons,
and all your holy people,
may we follow your paths in faith and hope
and radiate our joy and trust to all the world.

C. Jesus, Way to the Father

Almighty Father,
by our sharing in this mystery
enliven us with your Spirit
and conform us to the image of your Son.
Strengthen the bonds of our communion
with N. our pope, N. our bishop,
with all bishops, priests, and deacons,
and all your holy people.

Keep your Church alert in faith to the signs of the times
and eager to accept the challenge of the gospel.
Open our hearts to the needs of all humanity,
so that sharing their grief and anguish,
their joy and hope,
we may faithfully bring them the good news of salvation
and advance together on the way to your kingdom.

D. Jesus, the Compassion of God

Lord,
perfect your Church in faith and love
together with N. our pope, N. our bishop,
with all the bishops, priests, and deacons,
and all those your Son has gained for you.

Open our eyes to the needs of all;
inspire us with words and deeds
to comfort those who labour and are burdened;
keep our service of others
faithful to the example and command of Christ.

Let your Church be a living witness
to truth and freedom, to justice and peace,
that all people may be lifted up
by the hope of a world made new.

Be mindful of our brothers and sister [N. and N.],
who have fallen asleep in the peace of Christ,
and all the dead whose faith only you can know.
Lead them to the fullness of the resurrection
and gladden them with the light of your face.

When our pilgrimage on earth is complete,
welcome us into your heavenly home,
where we shall dwell with you for ever.
There, with Mary, the Virgin Mother of God,
with the apostles, the martyrs,
[Saint N.,] and all the saints,
we shall praise you and give you glory
through Jesus Christ, your Son.

Through him
with him
in him,
in the unity of the Holy Spirit,
all glory and honour is yours,
almighty Father,
for ever and ever.

Amen.

Latin Texts for the Mass

Confiteor
Confiteor Deo omnipotenti et vobis, fratres, quia
peccavi nimis
cogitatione, verbo, opere et omissione:
mea culpa, mea culpa, mea maxima culpa.
Ideo precor beatam Mariam semper Virginem,
omnes Angelos et Sanctos,
et vos, fratres, orare pro me
ad Dominum Deum nostrum.

Kyrie
Kyrie, eleison   **Kyrie, eleison.**
Christe, eleison.   **Christe, eleison.**
Kyrie, eleison.   **Kyrie, eleison.**

Gloria
Gloria in excelsis Deo
  et in terra pax hominibus bonae voluntatis.
Laudamus te, benedicimus te, adoramus te,
  glorificamus te,
gratias agimus tibi propter magnam
  gloriam tuam,
Domine Deus, Rex caelestis, Deus Pater
omnipotens.
Domine Fili unigenite, Jesu Christe,
Domine Deus, Agnus Dei, Filius Patris,
qui tollis peccata mundi, miserere nobis;
qui tollis peccata mundi, suscipe
  deprecationem nostram.
Qui sedes ad dexteram Patris, miserere nobis.
Quoniam tu solus Sanctus, tu solus Dominus,
  tu solus Altissimus,
Jesu Christe, cum Sancto Spiritu:
  in gloria Dei Patris.
  Amen.

Credo
Credo in unum Deum,
Patrem Omnipotentem, factorem caeli et terrae,
  visibilium omnium et invisibilium.
Et in unum Dominum Jesum Christum,
Filium Dei unigenitum, et ex Patre natum ante
  omnia saecula.
Deum de Deo, lumen de lumine, Deum verum
de Deo vero,
  genitum, non factum, consubstantialem Patri:
  per quem omnia facta sunt.
Qui propter nos homines et propter nostram
  salutem descendit de caelis.
Et incarnatus est de Spiritu Sancto ex Maria
  Virgine, et homo factus est.
Crucifixus etiam pro nobis sub Pontio Pilato;
  passus et sepultus est,

et resurrexit tertia die, secundum Scripturas,
  et ascendit in caelum, sedet ad dexteram Patris.
Et iterum venturus est cum gloria, iudicare
  vivos et mortuos, cuius regni non erit finis.
Et in Spiritum Sanctum, Dominum et
  vivificantem: qui ex Patre Filioque procedit.
Qui cum Patre et Filio simul adoratur
  et conglorificatur:
  qui locutus est per prophetas.
Et unam, sanctam, catholicam et apostolicam
  Ecclesiam.
Confiteor unum baptisma in remissionem
  peccatorum.
Et exspecto resurrectionem mortuorum,
  et vitam venturi saeculi. Amen.

Orate Fratres
Suscipiat Dominus sacrificium de manibus tuis
ad laudem et gloriam nominis sui,
ad utilitatem quoque nostram
totiusque Ecclesiae sanctae.

Sanctus
Sanctus, Sanctus, Sanctus Dominus Deus
  Sabaoth.
Pleni sunt caeli et terra gloria tua.
Hosanna in excelsis.
Benedictus qui venit in nomine Domini.
Hosanna in excelsis.

Pater noster
Praeceptis salutaribus moniti,
  et divina insitutione formati,
audemus dicere:

  Pater noster, qui es in caelis:
  sanctificetur nomen tuum;
    adveniat regnum tuum;
  fiat voluntas tua, sicut in caelo, et in terra.

  Panem nostrum cotidianum da nobis hodie;
  et dimitte nobis debita nostra,
    sicut et nos dimittimus debitoribus nostris
  et ne nos inducas in tentationem;
    sed libera nos a malo.

Agnus Dei
Agnus Dei, qui tollis peccata mundi:
  miserere nobis.
Agnus Dei, qui tollis peccata mundi:
  miserere nobis.
Agnus Dei, qui tollis peccata mundi:
  dona nobis pacem.